5/18

DATE DUE

W   R I

N I   C O

WITHDRAWN

PRINTED IN U.S.A.

Published by The History Press
Charleston, SC
www.historypress.net

First published 2017

Manufactured in the United States

ISBN 9781467135313

Library of Congress Control Number: 2016961486

This book is dedicated to the New Mexico soldiers who served the United States in the American Expeditionary Force during the First World War.

Contents

Foreword

D r. Daniel R. Cillis deserves great credit for having drafted a truly exceptional historical account of New Mexico's participation in World War I, or the "Great War," as it is commonly known. Most extraordinary is that no effort was spared in ensuring that every county in New Mexico is represented in firsthand accounts from the veterans themselves who entered service from each of our thirty-three counties.

As the author notes, many of our service members from New Mexico would participate in support of the Mexican Punitive Expedition, a prelude to World War I that, though unsuccessful in capturing Pancho Villa, served as a field laboratory as our forces experimented with new technologies such as aircraft and motorized transportation. Likewise, the author provides a one-of-a-kind window into the German Empire's strategy to influence American entry into the war through efforts to create a battlefront in the American Southwest. Eyewitness testimony revealed in the book shows that Pancho Villa's attack on Columbus, New Mexico, was partially motivated by such considerations.

New Mexicans would participate as soldiers, sailors and marines and serve in most if not all of the U.S. Army's wartime divisions. As such, they would see action in every battle undertaken by American forces. Most Americans view World War I as an event that took place on the Western Front (French and later occupation of German soil), but as Dr. Cillis points out, our doughboys would also serve in Siberia in support of the Eastern Front, where doughboys such as Anastacio Montoya of Santa Fe would be killed in action, as well as up the Yangtze River in China, in what was then called "Gunboat Diplomacy."

On the home front, Brigadier General James Baca, then adjutant general of the New Mexico National Guard, would lead recruitment efforts in a manner that would rank New Mexico fifth in the nation per capita in support of the war effort. New Mexico's home front Defense Councils would likewise lead the nation in their respective efforts.

Many of our doughboys would suffer serious injuries, such as Espiridion Lucero, Hijinio McCoy and Jose Leon Herrera of Cuba, New Mexico. New Mexico's Red Cross chapters would help families locate wounded doughboys who had been sent from the front to veteran hospitals throughout the nation for convalescent and rehabilitative care. In the case of Manuel Montoya of Corrales, New Mexico, it took the Red Cross two to three months of letter writing to hospitals throughout the nation to locate him at the hospital in Los Angeles. Upon his return, he started a family, but when his wounds reemerged, he was sent to the veterans' hospital in faraway Sheridan, Wyoming, where he remained until he died, as New Mexico at the time had no veterans' hospital. His story was by no means unique, as other families suffered similar experiences.

With more than eighty individual service member accounts, we become one with them as their lives are transformed on a journey from the quiet existence of farming or at home on the range herding cattle and sheep to the horrors of industrialized mass slaughter and chemical warfare. Most would never share their experiences with family upon their return. Many would suffer from what is now called Posttraumatic Stress Disorder (PTSD) without the benefit of services currently provided to our veterans. In this book, we remember and pay tribute to New Mexico's doughboy veterans and their families for their service and sacrifice for God and country. May we never forget the sacrifices they undertook to ensure our freedom and liberties.

This is a compelling book that honors the valor of New Mexico's residents in the Great War.

Respectfully,
DAVID C'DE BACA
Colonel, U.S. Army (Retired)

Acknowledgments

The author offers a special thanks to Colonel David C'de Baca, U.S. Army (Retired), for his highly substantive support and important contributions to *World War I New Mexico*. His enthusiasm for our great veterans is second to none. To Dr. Catherine Akel, Gary Herron and Nancy Maffucci, thank you for your support. Finally, I am grateful to the New Mexico doughboys who shared their stories and to all Americans who have worn our nation's uniform in maintaining our freedom.

Centenary

Initially, it was called the Great War. The First World War (1914–18) ended on the eleventh day of the eleventh month of 1918: Armistice Day. That truce, now observed in the United States as Veterans Day, may have faded from the collective consciousness. All those soldiers are gone; the war is beyond living memory. Yet the centenary years of the war remain a significant anniversary of a world-changing event. Milestones can enhance the power of the past in understanding current events. A thoughtful awareness of history can decipher the present and perhaps the future.

Although the centenary provided an incentive in writing this book, other factors blended in the creation of this project. It began while I was growing up in New York—and in a most unusual manner. Ensuing interest centered on how the First World War created sweeping changes in world politics and how repercussions have shaped much of today's global map.

Many current territorial conflicts and international relations can be better understood through the prism of the war. The sun began to set on the British Empire as the United States became a world power. Other empires— German, Turkish and Austro-Hungarian—dissolved. In the Middle East, new boundaries were created. Many resulting headlines—annexation, espionage, brutality, insurrection, invasion, totalitarianism and foreign intervention—have roots in the Great War. The First World War was the prologue for the Second World War, as well as for the Cold War, as the Soviet Union emerged as a twentieth-century power.

Interest in New Mexico began upon my arrival in Albuquerque and was significantly enhanced by my first trip to Santa Fe. New Mexico's culture, climate and history have had a lasting impact. The natural beauty of the desert/mountain landscapes and the grandeur of the architecture have been transformational. These experiences compelled me to become a resident of New Mexico. The U.S. territory, which became a state five years before the United States entered the war, lives up to the nickname that decorates automobile license plates: the "Land of Enchantment."

Researching the history of my adopted state and writing a historical novel about New Mexico statehood increased my awareness and provided additional perspectives. At that time, I discovered the long road from territory to statehood. It began in 1846 during the Mexican-American War, when the U.S. Army replaced the Mexican flag with the American flag in Santa Fe. After more than sixty years as a U.S. territory, New Mexico became the forty-seventh state. No other U.S. territory waited as long for statehood as New Mexico. Culture, religion and partisan politics were part of the barriers until President Taft signed the statehood bill on January 6, 1912.

Although New Mexico was a new state, military service was not a new initiative. The Santa Fe National Cemetery contains monuments to New Mexicans who served as soldiers in a long list of conflicts, including the Civil War and the Spanish-American War. A plaque in Albuquerque's Old Town Plaza describes a skirmish that led to Albuquerque being the Confederate capital of New Mexico. A Union victory at the Battle of Glorieta caused the Confederates to retreat to Texas. Overall, more than eight thousand soldiers from New Mexico served the Union cause.

The Rough Rider Memorial Museum in Las Vegas, New Mexico, presents further insight into the territory's military history. The museum tells the stories of the many New Mexicans who volunteered to serve in Cuba during the Spanish-American War. The Territory of New Mexico responded to the territorial governor's request and helped form units for the 1st United States Volunteer Cavalry—Roosevelt's Rough Riders. Graves of those who served in the Spanish-American War can be found in the Santa Fe National Cemetery. The cemetery is the burial place for nine Medal of Honor recipients and many World War I veterans. Given the World War I population of New Mexico—some 350,000 people—the state was well above the average of other states in supporting the war effort with military participation.

A century has passed since the First World War, and decades have passed since I heard an unusual story. The story—said to have happened in Corona,

New York, sometime in the summer of 1918—is how my interest in the war began. The following account is presented as narrative. Some details are clouded by time, but the essence of the story remains clear.

★★★

His olive drab uniform consisted of a tunic with four pockets, a high collar and shoulder straps. Tapered trousers were bound below the knees with leggings; his boots and belt were brown. Two small brass disks were pinned to the tunic choker—one with "US" and one with crossed rifles. A shoulder insignia with a red figure "1" was prominent.

At first glance, the soldier appeared exactly as he did on that day in France. A closer look would reveal a certain mysterious appearance. On the second floor of a modest house, he stood in a bedroom with two windows and a crying young boy.

The moment the child saw the soldier in his room, he stopped and stared in fear and then in fascination before asking, "Are you a soldier?"

"Yes, I am," he said from under a slightly cocked steel helmet. "Why are you crying?"

"I want my mommy and daddy," the boy replied. "They won't let me in their room."

"It's time for your own room."

"I don't want to be alone," the boy said, while rubbing his eyes.

"You are not alone. Look out that window; there is a good view of the park."

Crying again, the boy exclaimed, "I don't want to stay here!"

"Son, you are not alone here—you are with your imagination and you can go beyond sense and sight. You will think about your future. The heart of childhood will soar in this room and you will be happy."

"How do you know?" the boy whispered.

The soldier tried to bend down but could not. He was restricted to a position somewhere between attention and parade-rest. From that stance he said, "This was my room."

"Your room?"

"Yes, I was a boy in this room and imagined a future—but I had not a future. What you so forcefully reject is my most precious memory, all that remains of this room for me. Look out at the night and think about this room as your castle."

"Castle?"

"Yes, a castle! From which all things are possible. Imagination is important for understanding reality, not just fantasy."

Drying his eyes, the boy turned to the window, scanned the star-studded sky and viewed the small iron-fenced park. When he turned back, the soldier was gone.

This story may be fiction or may suggest that a home is a living memory of previous occupants. Whether or not the army doughboy appeared, there were additional details. As the story was told, the previous family in the apartment had a son who went to war and was among the first killed in the war. On May 31, 1918, near a small town in northern France, the doughboys engaged the German army. The ghost soldier in the Corona home was probably killed at the Battle of Cantigny, the first American battle of the war. The centenary, a ghost story, an ardent interest in history and a love of New Mexico converged to create this book about New Mexican doughboys.

Christmas Ceasefire

From the days of the Anasazis in Chaco Canyon to the Spanish in Santa Fe, the Wild West and the atomic laboratories, New Mexico has had a long and vivid history. New Mexico entered the Union in a time of world upheaval; the Great War started two years after statehood. Although Americans were aware of the state of world affairs, involvement with Germany was remote. Similarly, statehood affairs were more important to New Mexicans than world affairs. Yet the European conflicts would come to be significant for the new state.

The Great War, a bloodstained beginning to the twentieth century, ended any European optimism—especially in England, where a contented populace had cultural, political and economic confidence—and set a war-torn course for the following decades. Certainly, the "Long Edwardian Summer," perceived or real, was over.

Whether it was triggered by patriotism, nationalism, imperialism or a network of international alliances, the wildly impractical war demolished a generation. The major nations involved were France, Great Britain, Russia (the Triple Entente) and the United States. These Allies were opposed by Imperial Germany, Austria-Hungary and the Ottoman Empire, known as the Central Powers. Although it was a European conflict, the war extended to all continents, with the exception of Antarctica.

Today, that extraordinary period remains a monumental tragedy and a defining time as the deadliest war that the world has ever known. Five destructive years created an enduring record of murderous mayhem. The very words "trench warfare" conjure powerful images of deep mud, barbed wire, machine guns and artillery claiming ghastly casualties—more than double of all wars from 1790 to 1914. Battlefields such as the Somme and Verdun produced mass slaughters of young men. It was the first global conflict, and it changed warfare for all time.

As usual, advances in war machine technology outpaced military strategy and tactics. The Union army at Fredericksburg, Virginia, and the Confederate army at Gettysburg, Pennsylvania, suffered spectacularly deadly outcomes as Civil War weaponry surpassed prevailing military wisdom. Those battles were harbingers of a far greater disaster. Twentieth-century weapon industrialization and technology made the old method of trading lives for real estate extremely expensive. World War I casualties were ten times that of the U.S. Civil War. European armies had deadly artillery and machine guns; defensive fortifications extended battles for weeks. The armies became adept at developing new combat ways, thus continuing the war and increasing the costs. Advances in supply chains and reinforcement capabilities prolonged the killing. By contrast, Fredericksburg and Gettysburg were just hours and days in duration.

An examination the of Great War's death toll provides a stark look at the violence and slaughter that occurred. From a total of 65 million mobilized forces, there were 37 million casualties—8.5 million killed. Given the late entry of the United States into the war, American losses, though dreadful, were relatively low. The United States suffered 320,000 casualties, including 53,000 killed in action. Among that number are 501 New Mexicans.

Based on the cataclysmic event that claimed millions of lives, some observed an extreme pessimism about civilization. In view of the astonishing magnitude of destruction, it was argued that humans innately harbor violence and negative primitive instincts. Yet some soldiers were made to fight, and some were punished for fraternizing with the enemy.

The human violence theory was not supported on Christmas Eve 1914, when an amazing event occurred on the Western Front. British and German soldiers left their trenches to meet in no man's land, creating an informal truce. The opposing soldiers exchanged season's greetings, played football and even sang Christmas carols. Commanding generals from both sides ordered the Christmas Ceasefire to end—soldiers must focus on the business of killing. How can normally sane people inadvertently involve themselves in actions that result in war? Perhaps war defies logical explanation. In any case, after the devastating battles of 1915, any motivation to socialize with the enemy ended.

Five years after New Mexico entered the Union, the United States entered the war. About 4 million Americans from states across the country answered the call to serve, including citizens of the new state of New Mexico. U.S. soldiers who fought in World War I against the Central Powers have been recognized by their country. The purpose of this book is to recognize the New Mexican soldiers who were part of the American Expeditionary Force (AEF) led by General John "Black Jack" Pershing. The AEF was a deciding factor in winning the war.

This book explores the dramatic events and significant battles on the Western Front that preceded the U.S. entry into the war. The Southwest border conflicts, the AEF, the home front and the stories of more than eighty New Mexican doughboys are recounted.

In the following pages, American involvement in the war is described from a New Mexican perspective. *World War I New Mexico* tells the story of the state's soldiers who went "over there" and served in the Great War. The stories include all the counties and represent all the New Mexicans who served in 1917 and 1918. This work—which unites local, national and world history—is for those New Mexicans.

Chapter 1

The Great War

Across the Atlantic Ocean and six thousand miles away from Europe, New Mexico continued to develop as an American state, with William C. McDonald, from Upstate New York, as the first governor. Also in that year, the New Mexico Cattle Growers Association was established to advance the state's cattle industry. An assassination in a faraway place would ultimately stir New Mexico's patriotism.

The Great War began on June 28, 1914, with shots fired. Gavrilo Princip killed Archduke Franz Ferdinand and his wife, Sophie, in Sarajevo, Bosnia. Ferdinand was heir apparent to the Austro-Hungarian Empire. Princip was a Yugoslav nationalist. The assassin's objective was to free the Slav provinces from the empire and unify Yugoslavia as a state. Four days later, the bodies of the royal couple were returned to Vienna for a state funeral. The assassinations set off a series of actions and reactions heard throughout Europe.

From the Austro-Hungarian perspective, Serbia committed an intolerable act with the promise of further aggression. The Balkan region, boiling with political unrest, was close to open hostilities when the bullets hit their targets. Attacks had to be stopped or the empire's existence would be endangered. Austria-Hungary issued an ultimatum to Serbia containing draconian measures; it was a formality perhaps designed to justify an invasion.

Was this political calculation an opportunity for Germany to control Europe and challenge Great Britain for naval superiority? Germany conceivably used the Serbian crisis as a pretext to launch a war. Regardless, with German support, the empire leaders were ready to retaliate against the Serbs. Russia, aligned with Serbia, mobilized for action.

Accelerated change limited conciliation and consideration of the dire outcomes. Europe's leaders appeared to see truth as fixed and unchanging rather than determined by the consequences of ideas. This view together with narrow time frames prevented any balance between antipathy and humanity to emerge. Put differently, Europe was a continent obsessed with war and moving to the brink.

On July 28, Austria-Hungary declared war against Serbia and, before long, bombarded Belgrade. Days later, Germany and Russia exchanged declarations of war. France, based on a treaty with Russia, declared war on Germany. On August 3, Germany returned a declaration of war to France. Armies amassed on the borders, with Europe's map destined to become a battlefield diagram. Each European power believed it would rapidly win the war.

Assuredly, Austria-Hungary would defeat Serbia and seek revenge for the assassination. Germany expected little resistance in taking over France's industrial areas and capturing Paris. The Triple Entente had its perspectives, too. Great Britain believed that the Germans would be routed by year's end. France saw a chance to recapture Alsace-Lorraine, lost to the Germans in the 1870 war. The Franco-Prussian War was a degrading defeat for France; the result unified Germany with Prussian leadership and changed the balance of power. Russia would provide pressure on Germany from the east, thereby helping Great Britain and France achieve victory on the Western Front. Beyond the predictions, one thing was certain: the shooting in Sarajevo would lead to a world on fire.

It happened on August 3, 1914: German armies stormed through Belgium, starting the Great War. The German strategy was focused on avoiding the French border defenses and attacking through neutral Belgium at the town of Liège.

One day later, Great Britain reacted to the violation of Belgian neutrality by declaring war on Germany. Around the continent, events continued to spin out of control, with Germany declaring war on France and England. On August 7, the British Expeditionary Force (BEF) crossed the English

WORLD WAR I NEW MEXICO

Channel with six divisions and five cavalry brigades. Armies were on a collision course, with the outcome uncertain. Within one week, Europe moved from peace to all-out war.

In September, Germany marched on Paris with rapid advancement until stopped by a counteroffensive at the Battle of the Marne. As the Germans withdrew to the north, the British and French followed in what was called the "race to the sea." The northward advance from the Marne River to the North Sea laid the groundwork for the coming trench warfare and created the Western Front. About 2 million men fought in the opening battles, with an estimated 500,000 killed or wounded, ending any fantasy of a quick war. In October, the Germans captured Brussels and began bombing Antwerp. Surprisingly, the smaller Belgian army held the Germans at the Battle of Ypres.

Beyond the Western Front and within weeks, the Ottoman Empire declared a jihad against the Allies and entered the war with the Central Powers. There were five main battles in the Middle East, including the Sinai and the Palestine Campaigns. The Eastern Front spanned the frontier between Russia and Germany and from the Baltic Sea to the Black Sea. Given the thousand-mile front, the fighting was less entrenched, with more movement and repositioning. Germany achieved the first victory of the war with success at the Battle of Tannenberg, driving the Russians out of East Prussia. A second victory was achieved at Battle of the Masurian Lakes. However, both Germany and Austria-Hungary had lost territory on the Eastern Front by year's end.

Meanwhile, on the Western Front, many believed that the war would be over by December. Yet the war was far from over: the kaiser's army did not conquer France, and heavy losses were sustained as the opposing armies became embedded into long defensive lines. It was an introduction to the grim realities of trench warfare. Failed plans by German and French army commanders created a lethal deadlock.

At the start of 1915, Germany's new zeppelin airships attacked English coastal towns, killing civilians. Then the "big cigars in the sky" were used for reconnaissance. When the war started, aero planes provided little more than reconnaissance. Then air power on both sides engaged in strategic bombing of factories, dockyards and power plants, as well as of tactical targets such as supply lines. Zeppelin bases in Cologne and Dusseldorf were attacked in British air raids.

Spring carried a hideous new weapon to the battlefield: chlorine gas. German gas bombs fired on Allied trenches caused many survivors to run from an unimaginable horror. Soon after, the Allies produced gas masks and a warning system. A screaming fog horn signaled the men to put on their masks. Then the Allies launched their own gas attacks, only to be faced with another horrifying weapon that projected a stream of fire: the flamethrower.

Action on the North Atlantic was dominated by German submarine attacks on supply ships. The submarine strategy of isolating Great Britain from the United States was successful in its operation—perhaps too successful in regard to civilian ships. This was profoundly illustrated by the sinking of the ocean liner *Lusitania*. In May, the ship was sailing from New York to Liverpool when it was torpedoed by a German U-boat. The attack killed more than 2,000 passengers, including 128 Americans, and moved the U.S. public opinion toward war. New York newspapers called the sinking of the *Lusitania* murder and condemned the Germans. Theodore Roosevelt denounced the sinking as piracy.

The world changed with the attack; there were no longer hard rules of war. Even so, the United States remained on the sidelines, adhering to President Wilson's goal to stay out of the foreign war. Besides, going to war over the sinking of a British ship with a British flag was not a clear choice (the *Lusitania* was also transporting millions of cartridges and thousands of shrapnel shells to be used against the German army).

Germany had warned the U.S. public that traveling on a British ship flying the British flag had serious risks. A notice in the *New York Times* informed the American passengers, but they may have been unaware of the munitions on board the *Lusitania*. Despite American neutrality, Wilson did protest the infamous attack on the *Lusitania*. He demanded German assurance that the U-boats would stop attacking, prompting the Germans to comply—or so it seemed.

In August 1914, the British choked off supplies to Germany. In reaction to Britain's naval blockade, Germany accelerated its submarine strategy to stop transatlantic supply shipments, and in time, it conducted unhampered submarine warfare. By October, U-boats had sunk 1 million tons of supplies on the Atlantic and attacked Allied ships near Nantucket Island.

The ongoing deadlock and increased death counts on the Western Front pressed the Allies to seek alternatives to victory. Attacking the Central Powers from the Black Sea to conquer Constantinople was thought to be a solid strategy. In April, the Allies invaded the Ottoman Empire on the beaches of the Gallipoli, the north bank of the Dardanelles strait, which provides access to Russia.

In an attempt to capture the strait, a naval and amphibious assault was conducted. The Allies found landing areas on the peninsula to be heavily defended by Turkish troops. Over a period of months, French and British troops were stopped as they slammed against fortified hills, losing forty-three thousand men and failing to take the peninsula. Gallipoli was an Allied disaster. An order to withdraw was issued in December; the operation was abandoned in January. Elsewhere in 1915, Serbia and Montenegro were conquered, the Italian campaigns were indecisive and Lawrence of Arabia led an Arab revolt against Turkey.

After the first full year of fighting on the Western Front, little military gains were accrued by the Triple Entente or the Central Powers. The only gains of the campaigns were hard lessons that massed infantry charges were obsolete and suicidal. Despite staggering loss of life, the Allied high command was planning another large-scale offensive to drive the Germans from the Western Front.

By 1916, Austria-Hungary, Bulgaria, Germany and the Ottoman Empire were battling Britain, France, Russia, Italy, Belgium, Serbia, Montenegro and Japan. The longest and most costly battle of the war occurred at Verdun, France. In February, the battle began with German artillery shelling French positions and ended with massive death tolls for all the combatant armies.

In the United States, Pancho Villa and his army raided Columbus, New Mexico (see chapter 3), sending General John Pershing and the U.S. Army into Mexico to pursue Villa. It was a prelude to Pershing and the American army fighting in France.

In May, the naval battle of Jutland raged. Warships of the Royal Navy and of the Imperial German Navy clashed in the North Sea near Denmark. It was the greatest and the only major naval battle of the war. The two great fleets, some two hundred ships, fought to an indecisive end, yet the Royal Navy remained in control of the North Sea.

In July, the British fired hundreds of thousands of shells at German positions, attempting to help the French at Verdun and starting the Battle of the Somme. Under a barrage of return fire, the British sustained more than twenty thousand casualties in mere hours. Both battles came to an end in the final weeks of the year. The Somme introduced the first tank in warfare and is remembered for the key role of artillery, the war in the sky, shell shock and desertion.

In 1917, the Russian Revolution would eventually end the fighting on the Eastern Front. Germany openly announced its North Atlantic submarine campaign and resumed U-boat attacks on ships sailing to Britain, including American ships. Perhaps the Germans were overconfident that the United States would not enter the war. Certainly, an ocean dominated by U-boats could hamper the arrival of the U.S. forces in France. However, it was a gross miscalculation. The U.S. response was to design a convoy system for protection of Allied shipments to Europe. German submarines were overpowered by the escort vessels, thereby ending Germany's victories at sea and moving the United States closer to war.

In this country, President Wilson ordered General John Pershing to end the pursuit of Pancho Villa in Mexico and redeploy U.S. troops along the border. Since the *Lusitania* disaster, tensions between the United States and Germany were escalating. Then, in an astonishing German affront, Berlin threatened the United States through the Zimmermann Telegram (see chapter 4), which offered a military alliance with Mexico. Mexico was encouraged to enter World War I as an ally to the Central Powers and attack the United States. The offer was disregarded by Mexico but not by President Wilson.

In April, Congress declared war on Germany. It was a world-shaking event for America. Britain and France needed U.S. reinforcements and, in large measure, welcomed the United States into the war. Under the command of General Pershing, the AEF would take to the battlefields and turn the tide of the war in favor of the Allies. Ultimately, 2 million U.S. doughboys would go to France, including thousands of soldiers from New Mexico.

Although the new state was geographically and historically isolated, it would rise to the occasion to share the burden of America. New Mexico mobilized its resources, without reservation, in response to the U.S. call to arms.

In May 1918, the final year of the war, the Treaty of Brest-Litovsk ended the war on the Eastern Front. In March 1918, Lenin's Bolshevik government of Soviet Russia signed the treaty with the Central Powers. As a result, the Central Powers controlled territory from the Baltic to Ukraine; Germany redeployed eastern armies to engage the Allies in the Spring Offensive.

In May, the first U.S. engagement in World War I occurred at the Battle of Cantigny, in northern France. The 1st Division of the AEF, in reserve for the French army, was successful in the battle. In August, Austrian officials announced that their country would seek a separate peace with the Allies. In July, Czar Nicholas and his family were killed by Bolsheviks as the Russian Revolution cost 15 million lives. In the spring and summer, the long sustained attacks of the Hundred Days Offensive produced failure after failure for the German army. In the fall, the Central Powers began to unravel. Bulgaria surrendered, and the Austro-Hungarian Empire ended.

German involvement on the U.S.-Mexican border came to light again when the U.S. Army Signal Corps at Fort Huachuca, Arizona, became aware of German military advisors in Sonora, Mexico, and began surveillance. A tangle between a Mexican gun smuggler and U.S. Custom agents escalated into the Battle of Nogales.

Doughboys were vital at the Second Battle of the Marne, the Battle of St. Mihiel and the Battle of the Argonne Forest. These battles—with the American army involved—proved to be decisive for the Allies. The weight of Allied armies and resources battered the German invaders' ability to hold their ground. With the support for the war crumbling in Berlin, Kaiser Wilhelm escaped from Germany. Then, on a cool fall day, the last chapter of that history unfolded in France. Fighting would end at the eleventh hour on November 11, 1918—Armistice Day.

The armistice ended the war for the doughboys in Europe but not for all the men. Thousands of U.S. troops were in Siberia—a little-known chapter of World War I. After the armistice, the American troops faced a very harsh winter there. In July 1918, Wilson sent General William S. Graves, commander of the AEF in Siberia, and almost ten thousand men to the town of Vladivostok. Red and White Russians were marauding Siberia and seeking to control the Trans-Siberian Railway. The Americans protected this key railway line and found many locals supporting the Bolsheviks, and many others sought U.S protection. Cossacks ruthlessly attacked the doughboys guarding the railway as the United States became a target.

Also, Japanese involvement in Russian territory and a Czech Legion in danger of attack by the Red Army in Siberia were issues that concerned Wilson. There also was a matter of 500,000 tons of unprotected war materiel that was vulnerable to plundering.

Frank Beaman of Albuquerque arrived in Vladivostok, Siberia, from the Philippines in September 1918. He was with Company D, 31st Infantry Regiment, the so-called Polar Bear Regiment, which lost thirty men, with some fifty men wounded. Sixteen soldiers received the Distinguished Service Cross. This award, created in World War I, is the second-highest combat award given for extraordinary bravery in action against an enemy. Doughboy Frank Beaman's impression of Siberia is reflected in his own words: "[I] hate to see this country importing arms and ammunition….The population is split up into factions just like it was in Old Mexico and whichever side or faction gets the arms they are quite liable to be used against American soldiers as not." In December 1918, Beaman happily returned to the United States and offered his appreciation: "The sensation of getting back to America is almost worthwhile spending a year in Siberia."

Harvey Herron of Colfax County enlisted in the army in the summer of 1917. After spending time stationed in Fort Logan, Colorado; Angel Island, California; and Manilla, Philippines, he departed for Siberia. On August 14,

Harvey Herron.

1918, he was assigned to patrolling and guarding the Trans-Siberian Railway. The job lasted until November 11, 1919, a full year after the war ended.

Beyond enduring a brutal winter of sixty degrees below zero, Herron and his patrol were engaged against Kraviska bandits. Just 14 Americans clashed with 120 bandits, but it was a decisive win for the doughboys—16 bandits were killed, with 4 taken prisoner. The army patrol lost a single man.

Doughboy Herron reflected on his time in the army. He expressed a positive view and his happiness to serve his county to the best of his ability. Having seen a great deal of the world, he always remembered his time in the army.

Pete Castillo, from the town of Mimbres in Grant County, New Mexico, left the Presidio in San Francisco in September 1918. He was in Siberia three weeks later. His unit, Company D, 31st Infantry, skirmished with the Red Guards in May and July 1919. Doughboy Castillo remained in Siberia until January 1920.

When the White Russians were defeated, the American intervention in Siberia was over. More than three hundred American soldiers were lost, including New Mexicans Nester Lopez of Socorro County, who was killed in action on June 25, 1919, and Anastacio Montoya of Santa Fe County, who died of wounds on July 5, 1919. By April 1920, all the U.S soldiers had left Siberia, the suffering and the forgotten war.

Chapter 2

The Western Front

1914–1916

Flanders Fields refers to major World War I battlefields in the Belgian provinces of Flanders and of Nord-Pas-de-Calais in France. Flanders is especially remembered for the Battles of the Ypres Salient and Passchendaele. Battle lines encompassed France, Belgium, Luxembourg and Germany—the Western Front.

The Western Front is symbolized by shocking trench warfare within scarred, shattered terrain. Both armies built opposing trench fortifications from the North Sea to the French border with Switzerland. The four-hundred-mile front was heavy with barbed wire and machine gun nests; the territory between the lines was known as no man's land.

When men went "over the top" of the trenches, they climbed up with weapons and equipment and moved out over broken ground filled with wire and imminent death. Instinctively, the men made themselves as small a target as possible in the face of rifle and machine gun fire. Soldiers who made it to the German trenches engaged in a direct attack in an attempt to capture the position. However, in most cases, the attacks resulted in high casualty rates.

Although soldiers were rotated in and out of the front lines, time in the infamous trenches was pure misery. In addition to defending against raids and attacks, soldiers were faced with gas, snipers and large trench rats that did not care if they ate the dead or the living. Living in the trenches within restricted spaces and under brutal conditions caused extreme stress, disease and death.

Despite many attacks and counterattacks on the Western Front, battle lines changed little throughout the war, with the cost of small gains measured in large death tolls. Even mounted troops, with a mobility and speed advantage over infantry, were unable to achieve success against the new military methods. The elite European cavalry units were continually unsuccessful on the front line. Battlefield conditions, barbed wire, machine guns and tanks reduced the cavalry's usefulness and forced it into history. This provided evidence that cavalry was obsolete—except for the 2nd U.S. Cavalry Regiment (see chapter 5).

1914

In August 1914, Germany initialized the Schlieffen Plan to defeat France and Russia and win the war. The plan was designed by former German chief of staff Alfred von Schlieffen, who warned against fighting on two fronts at the same time. That risk would be reduced by attacking France before a Russian offensive. After success on the Western Front, the Germans would focus on the Eastern Front: first France and then Russia.

According to plan, Germany invaded Luxembourg, Belgium and regions of northern France with greater German troop strength than that of the Allies. In Liège, Belgium, a heavy howitzer bombardment caused the defenders to retreat to Antwerp. However, French fortifications stalled the German invasion. Soon after, the BEF under General Sir John French arrived in France and engaged the German army at the Battle of the Frontiers. French was chief of staff of the British army and was promoted to field marshal in 1913. This resulted in a British retreat to the Marne River. The retreating army conducted gritty rear guard operations and was prepared to fight another day.

By September, the Schlieffen Plan was destroyed. A major Allied counteroffensive dramatically stopped the invasion. The British and French met the Germans at the first Battle of the Marne—an Allied success in terms of stopping the German advance near the Marne River. Overall, the German plan for a quick win was over: they were denied Paris and overall victory.

Despite the Allies' strategic success, the German army was far from defeated. Then the Allies pressed their advantage, however late, with an offensive against the retreating Germans at the First Battle of the Aisne. The

BEF and the French army crossed the Aisne River in darkness. Then heavy artillery and machine guns destroyed the landscape and created a dreadful impasse that would lead to a long-term stalemate.

Eventually, the leadership on both sides realized that mass frontal assaults were madness. Sickening heavy losses, measured in the hundreds of thousands, led to a strategy change to smaller, tactical flanking movements. That set the stage for the "race to the sea" and created longer lines of trenches—some four hundred miles from Belgium through France and to Switzerland. Overall, the Allies saved Paris and established a stalemate on the Western Front—but not an armistice. The Germans bombed Antwerp, leading to an Allied evacuation of the city and to fighting on the Yser River in French Flanders.

In October, the struggle to control the Belgian city of Ypres began. Ypres was significantly strategic: if the Allied line collapsed, French ports on the English Channel could be captured. Obtaining this advantageous position would be a major German victory, paving the way for invading England.

British, Belgian and French forces clashed with German armies on an epic scale with 1 million soldiers. In the end, the Allied armies resisted the German attack; there was no breakthrough for the kaiser's men and no invasion of England. The month-long battle left both sides with massive losses—a stunning death total of 75,000 men, including almost half of the British army. During the battle, inexperienced German student-soldiers marched into a killing field. The disaster was called the "massacre of the innocents." The Germans were held at the Battle of Ypres, a front that remained basically unchanged for the duration of the war.

The Belgian army held the German advance near the Yser River, albeit with heavy losses. When the smoke cleared in November, the Ypres Salient was established and would become a highly contested scene of brutal fighting. A salient, a protrusion in a defensive line, can be attacked from three sides and can be an exposed positon for soldiers in place there. Relief arrived in the winter; the armies settled in their respective trenches and ceased fire.

1915

In the winter of 1915, the deadlock hardened with the terrain. The established trenches, from the Belgian coast to the Swiss border, were solidified. The strategy of the British and French high command was simple: drive the Germany army from Flanders. Undeniably, the Germans controlled regions in Flanders that contained raw materials and heavy industry. Also, German trench weapons of mortars, grenades and heavy guns had a decisive advantage over those of the Allies. Allied forces were stopped by the Germans from strong entrenched positions with barbed wire and deadly machine guns. For these reasons, the British and French strategy failed.

The "Champagne Offensive" dominated the war news on the Western Front until March 1915. Fought in the Champagne region of France, it started in December 1914 as the first major offensive against the Germans since the construction of trenches. The French were met with strong resistance by enemy lines that were well prepared for defensive warfare. Initially, the French offensive was halted in the face of a German counterattack. The Allies had marginal gains with heavy losses and failed to destroy the railway supplying the Germans.

In mid-March, British forces assaulted the German lines at Neuve Chapelle, a French village close to the Belgian border. Before the battle, the Royal Flying Corps used air reconnaissance to create detailed maps of the German trenches. This scouting and the resulting accurate bombardment from 340 big guns shocked the Germans. The Great War was an artillery war; the feared guns killed on a wide scale and inflicted dreadful injuries. In France, the British artillery regiments contained horse artillery and field artillery.

The Germans withstood the opening artillery barrage only to be faced with British and Indian infantry attacks. The lack of effective communication between the British front lines and the commanders in the field caused confusion and mistakes in deploying troops and guns. However, there was enough Allied penetration to capture Neuve Chapelle and the salient near the town.

In April, the Germans used massive clouds of chlorine gas on French troops near the Ypres Salient, killing thousands of men in minutes. The unprotected French divisions retreated in an understandable state of panic. Ironically, the Germans were reluctant to press their advantage given the looming gas clouds. During this Second Battle of the Ypres, the Germans used poison gas four more times. In May, the battle ended with the Ypres Salient taking the shape it would maintain for two years. Of course, once again the fight resulted in heavy casualties.

Throughout the year, the BEF gained substantial strength, with new armies and divisions, including the 2nd Canadian Division. Then, in the fall, the Second Battle of Champagne began with the French flying flags and playing "La Marseillaise." A heavy bombardment preceded and aided the French infantry's advance. The Germans offered formidable resistance to the offensive and ended the French plan.

By year's end, the defensive fortifications had improved in complexity and in effectiveness. Both sides lost tens of thousands of soldiers with little change in the battle lines. Yet there was a change of command within the BEF: General Sir Douglas Haig replaced General Sir John French. It was believed that Haig would lead the BEF with greater professionalism.

1916

In February 1916, the German high command implemented its planned knockout blow against the staggering French. The battle site was the French fortress-city of Verdun. As the city was a source of national pride, and given its rich culture and significant history, the French army would not abandon Verdun.

The root of Verdun was in the First Battle of the Marne, which stopped the German invasion of France. As a result, the Germans dug in with complex and strong defensive positions to maintain the captured territory. The French reacted with siege warfare in an effort to retake the territory. However, the offensives of the two previous years resulted in little territorial gain and large loss of life.

In the Battle of Verdun, the French and German armies engaged in bloody combat in the hills of northeastern France. On February 21, the town of Verdun suffered a massive German bombardment. The French lost surrounding defensive positions and large numbers of men but dealt the Germans large losses as well. Railway lines to Verdun were severed by the German artillery. This left Voie Sacrée as the only reliable road remaining to supply the army; it connected Bar-le-Duc to Verdun.

The German strategy rested on the belief that the French would react to the offensive with a counteroffensive. A German attack at Région Fortifiée de Verdun would take Côtes de Meuse. From that high ground, powerful artillery fire from secure German positions would be deadly. The Germans believed that the counterattacks would destroy the French strategic reserves and force France to seek peace.

As always, military strategy is as good as the first shot fired. As the battle raged for months, commanders of both armies were obsessed with attacks, creating monstrous cycles of slaughter—the madness continued as no commander wanted to be the first to stop. At the least, the French recaptured much of the ground lost and contained the Germans.

At the end of ten months, from February to December, the long and grave struggle at Verdun claimed more than 700,000 combined French and German casualties. In the end, there was no real advantage to either side. Verdun, considered the greatest and longest battle in history, was a strategic failure given the appalling losses and the continuation of the war. Much of the German failure is attributed to the movement of artillery and infantry from Verdun as reinforcements for the Somme when the British launched an offensive to help the French.

After the Gallipoli failure, the British high command continued to focus on the Western Front for victory. Russia would attack from the north and the south. Britain and France would attack near the River Somme. The Allied high command disagreed on the practicality of such a high-risk plan. Previously, massive offensives had proved to be unsuccessful. Moreover, German defensive lines were continually improving with more trenches, barbed wire and machine guns. The Allies were not yet strong enough for a new offensive. Nevertheless, the plan that was approved by British commander in chief Haig was placed in motion. The German Verdun offensive would change the purpose and date of the Somme plan.

The offensive, along a twenty-mile front located north of the Somme River near Arras, was designed to force the Germans to move assets from Verdun to defend the Somme. When the Germans attacked Verdun, inflicting heavy casualties, the British accelerated the plan, primarily based on French demands. First, a massive infantry attack would soften up the German lines; this would be followed by a massed cavalry charge that would break the German lines. That was the plan, the theory. The battle line from the North Sea to the Swiss border, held by Germany since the start of the war, would be parted, allowing the cavalry to enter to finish the job—provided that all would go well.

All did not go well. It began with a heavy bombardment of the German lines with the intent to silence their machine guns. It did not. Heavily fortified trenches allowed the Germans to answer the attack in a strong way. The whistles blew at 0700 hours on the morning of July 1, 1916; British divisions went "over the top" and moved across no man's land. German machine guns opened up, cutting down the British soldiers. German guns killed more than twenty thousand men; another thirty-eight thousand were wounded— it was the largest single-day loss for the British army.

Despite the British artillery firing more than 1 million explosive and gas shells, the remaining Germans destroyed the British plan by inflicting 58,000 casualties on one day. The Battle of the Somme became synonymous with slaughter; it was a great catastrophe for the British at 400,000 casualties. In addition, there were 200,000 French and 650,000 German casualties. The British did relieve the French at Verdun, in a small measure of success.

The battle ended in November with the Allies advancing only a few miles. As 1916 came to an end, the bloody stalemates would be remembered as the year the Germans tried to destroy the French army at Verdun and the year the British tried to break through at the Somme. Both great ideas ended in failure. The war would stagger on for two more years with more heavy losses.

In the United States, President Wilson won a second term, defeating Charles Hughes. He was reelected with the slogan "He kept us out of war." That campaign promise would be soon broken.

Chapter 3

Columbus, New Mexico

March 1916

On the North American side of the Atlantic, revolution continued in Mexico with Francisco "Pancho" Villa as commander of the Constitutionalist army. A year before the United States entered the First World War, an act of war occurred in New Mexico. The incident, rooted in the internal affairs of the chaotic Mexican Revolution, had a complex connection to Germany.

In 1915, Mexican leader Victoriano Huerta sought to have favorable relations with America, especially American business. Beyond the economic issues, the United States was uninterested in Mexico's internal politics; Washington even discouraged U.S. citizens from providing aid to any party to the Mexican civil war. In New Mexico, there was neutrality conflict that made headlines. Lawyer Elfego Baca represented Huerta's government in the United States. He also represented General José Salazar, who was charged with smuggling arms into Mexico. Baca was charged with aiding Salazar in escaping from a New Mexican jail. Baca was acquitted.

American neutrality was consistent until President Wilson objected to Huerta's killing of his political enemies, including predecessor Francisco Madero. Consequently, Wilson supported Mexican Revolutionary generals Villa and Venustiano Carranza in their opposition to Huerta and to each other. During this time, German agents may have had a relationship with Huerta. There was no concrete proof of German involvement with Huerta or of plotting with him against the United States, but the Zimmermann Telegram (see chapter 5) was definitive proof of German intervention.

In April, a twist of fate intervened when Mexican soldiers arrested U.S. sailors thought to be intruding in Tampico, Mexico. Although they were quickly released, the Tampico incident strained diplomatic relations between the United States and Mexico. Then, the United States demanded that an American flag be raised on Mexican land. Wilson responded by sending the U.S. Navy's Atlantic Fleet to Veracruz, supposedly to block a German shipment of arms to Huerta.

A chain of events increased the tension and caused the U.S. ships to attack the city. The Atlantic Fleet conducted an amphibious assault and engaged in a street battle before occupying the port city. This invasion at Veracruz helped Carranza win the support of the Mexican people and oust Huerta. Once in power, Carranza opposed the United States. The chaos continued with the revolutionary generals pitted against each other, and Wilson's recognition of Carranza as the Mexican leader infuriated Villa.

In November 1915, Villa blamed the United States for helping the *federales* at Agua Prieta and at Hermosillo. At Agua Prieta, he claimed that U.S. soldiers used searchlights during the battle. At the Battle of Hermosillo, the *federales* moved troops via American railways.

With animosity for the United States, Villistas attacked a train in Chihuahua, killed eighteen American passengers and initiated a series of raids along the U.S.-Mexican border. Then, with his vision of leading Mexico fading and his army in need of supplies, Villa invaded New Mexico. Perhaps it was a blatant attempt to entangle the United States in a full-blown war with Mexico. At any rate, on March 9, 1916, Villa and his armed force crossed the border and raided New Mexico.

Villa and about five hundred mounted men charged into the border town of Columbus, New Mexico. The small town of Columbus was home to Americans and Mexicans, and the 13th U.S. Calvary was garrisoned at nearby Camp Furlong. The raiders burned buildings and businesses and stole guns and horses. In the end, Villa's men sustained many casualties and were forced to retreat by three hundred cavalry troopers, but not before damaging the town and killing eighteen townspeople and thirty-seven U.S. soldiers. When the smoke had cleared, Villa's invasion of Columbus caused public outcry for retribution, and the U.S. Army moved closer to action.

The National Guard, under state governor control, can be called into federal control by the president to increase the strength of the regular army. The National Defense Act of 1916 called up National Guard units that were stationed on the Mexican border. Also, Wilson answered the attack by ordering a small army into Mexico to capture or kill Villa. Secretary of War Newton Baker organized a military expedition, with General Pershing chosen to command the army at Camp Furlong. The U.S. Army, which had authority to pursue any hostiles who raided American territory into Mexico, quickly made preparations to conduct the Mexican Punitive Expedition to capture Villa. Troops, supplies and armored motor vehicles poured into the newly established command post in Columbus, which was still recovering from the raid. The expedition was assembled in Columbus and at Culberson's Ranch in New Mexico. Units of the expedition included infantry regiments, cavalry regiments, field artilleries, aero squadrons, engineers, ambulance companies and a Signal Corps company. New Mexico National Guard units were stationed on the Mexican border and upstate at Truth or Consequences, New Mexico. They provided help for Mexican refugees, guarded captured Villistas and prepared armaments.

The Columbus raid story had another perspective from Maude Wright, who was kidnapped by Villa. She reported that Villa raided New Mexico to provoke the Germans to intervene. On March 1, 1916, Wright was kidnapped by Villa's men from her ranch and family in northern Mexico. She rode north with Villa to the U.S. border for one hundred miles and learned of their plan to attack Columbus. During the attack, she was a prisoner in Villa's camp. When Villa retreated, she was set free and rode into Columbus.

By April 8, 1916, Pershing was hundreds of miles inside Mexico with six thousand regular army soldiers in the pursuit of Villa. There were separate skirmishes involving U.S. troops and Villa's men, as well as with Carranza's men. Despite covering hundreds of miles of mountains and deserts, even with aircraft, the Mexican leader remained elusive.

Reminiscent of the Mexican-American War, the Pershing invasion caused Villa's army to increase in size and in spirit and brought the two countries to the brink of war. However, events in Europe overshadowed any public appetite for war with Mexico, if it existed at all. Besides, Villa was not the legitimate Mexican leader.

Then, with U.S.-Mexico relations deteriorating, Carranza requested that Pershing withdraw from Mexico. In February 1917, as part of a negotiated settlement, U.S. troops discontinued the chase and departed Mexico; the Mexican government would answer for raids on American towns. As a defense against further raids, regular army soldiers conducted border patrols and guarded the U.S.-Mexico border. Wilson ordered the National Guard into federal service to reinforce garrisons on the border; guardsmen were placed in San Antonio, El Paso, Nogales and Brownsville. The New Mexican National Guard served on the border from May 1916 until April 1917.

In the end, Villa was not captured and was able to direct all his aggression against the Carranza government. The Mexican Punitive Expedition ended unsuccessfully two months before the United States declared war on Germany, with France a likely destination for Pershing's men. The foreign adventure provided military experience for the U.S. forces, both regular army and guardsmen. In essence, the expedition trained the men for World War I and may have allowed the United States to enter the war sooner than later. Many of the men who served in Mexico served in France. Likewise, many New Mexicans who served on the border also served in France. Similarly, General Pershing's experience in Mexico led to his promotion as commander of the AEF in Europe. The Columbus raid story appeared in a local newspaper of the Public Service Company of New Mexico:

> *ELECTRIC LINES, PUBLIC SERVICE CO. OF NEW MEXICO*
> *Volume 16, Number 4, 1916*
>
> *It's four-thirty in the morning on March 9, 1916. Suddenly the early morning stillness is shattered by cries of "Villa! Villa!" and 500 of General Francisco "Pancho" Villa's "Villistas" storm to the attack of Columbus and nearby Camp Furlong. Troopers of the 13th Cavalry from Camp Furlong quickly respond to the attack. Maneuvering through the camp and village, they set up machine guns and pour a deadly cross-fire at the raiders. For an hour a half the battle rages, but by dark the "Villistas," sensing defeat, retreat toward the border. The battle is over.*
>
> *Why Villa decided to attack a U.S. town—particularly one with soldiers stationed nearby—is unclear. But in the aftermath of that raid, the area around Columbus saw a military extravaganza lasting for eleven months. Led by General John J. "Blackjack" Pershing, the U.S. Army fielded an expedition to capture Villa. They never caught Villa but the expedition did feature several military milestones, including the first large-scale use of mechanized vehicles. Here trucks and cars saw their first military use, and fragile 90 hp Curtiss biplanes took off from Columbus to scout the desert terrain. But perhaps the most important, the Pershing expedition proved to be an invaluable experience for the men involved, many of whom found themselves a few months later in the trenches of France.*

In March 2016, the town of Columbus, New Mexico, observed the centenary of the Pancho Villa raid.

Chapter 4

The Zimmermann Affair

January 1917

Columbus, New Mexico, is a long way from Germany, but the Villa raid and the Pershing expedition did not escape the attention of the leadership in Berlin. Germany's interest in the United States turned to the Southwest, rather than the Western Front. There was an opportunity to leverage the strained U.S.-Mexico relations combined with the Mexican-American War territorial legacy. A message was sent from Berlin to Mexico City in the context of increased border tensions.

It began in January 1917, when the British intercepted German foreign minister Arthur Zimmermann's coded message intended for the German ambassador to Mexico, Heinrich von Eckardt. The telegram contained an explosive message: if the United States entered the war, Mexico would declare war on the nation. Germany offered financial support and a military alliance—one that required Mexico to attack the United States in the Southwest. In this way, U.S. involvement in the European war would continue to be limited to supplying materiel. Also, if the United States entered the war, Mexico could weaken the Americans in France by engaging the United States in a new border war. In return, Mexico's lost Southwest territories would revert to Mexico. In that unlikely scenario, Germany would support Mexico's conquest of the Southwest, and Texas, New Mexico and Arizona would revert to Mexico. It was a grand case of overreaching.

Unknown to Germany, the coded message was intercepted by British agents. To prevent Germany from learning that the code was compromised, the British did not reveal the interception. Eventually, American agents in

London deciphered the code and presented the message to President Wilson. It was believed that the British gave the note to the Americans expecting the message to cause the United States to enter the war. It was also believed by some that the telegram was created by the British. However, Zimmermann said that the telegram was genuine.

The message was published in the *New York Times* and widely publicized in U.S. newspapers. Public opinion against Germany increased, much to the satisfaction of the British. The story became public following the end of the Mexican Punitive Expedition. The Zimmermann Affair highlighted the interaction among U.S. and German governments and tied the Mexican Revolution to the war in Europe. This fueled the narrative of a Mexico/Germany alliance. This secret telegram did not have the same dramatic impact or awareness of the sinking of the *Lusitania*, yet it moved the United States closer to war. In fact, Zimmermann's overture to the Carranza government in Mexico City inflamed American public opinion. To that point, America remained on an isolationist footing, but that would not be for long.

In August, Wilson officially stated the U.S. policy of neutrality in an address to Congress, warning Americans against a breach of neutrality. Most Americans supported the position of avoiding foreign wars, but that would change. Public opinion began to change in reaction to events, and then the United States severed diplomatic ties with Germany.

Wilson addressed Congress about the attacks on U.S. property and citizens and the resumption of Atlantic U-boat attacks. American Merchant Marine ships were armed in response. Then three U.S. merchant ships were sunk by U-boats. This and the action indicated in the telegram were enough. The Zimmermann Affair was considered a breaking point for America's neutrality and directly led to America's entry into the First World War.

All this led to a U.S. declaration of war against Germany on April 2, 1917. President Wilson argued before a special session of Congress that the U-boat war was against all nations. His position that America must help make the world safe for democracy came to be realized when Congress voted to approve the declaration of war on Germany. Subsequently, war was also declared against Austria-Hungary but not against the Ottoman Empire. American doughboys would focus on the fight in France and, to a lesser degree, in Russia.

German involvement in U.S. and Mexican affairs may have gone beyond the Zimmermann Telegram. It was speculated that Germany was the author of the "Plan of San Diego." This 1915 Spanish document advocated an invasion designed to recapture the lands ceded to the United States after the 1846 Mexican-American War. The goal of the unnamed authors was the creation of another Mexican republic consisting of U.S. Southwest territories. The San Diego Plan was discovered by American authorities in Texas. It called for coups in California, Arizona, New Mexico and Texas. Except for raids into Texas, the plan never occurred, but it shocked U.S. authorities, providing further suspicion between the two countries.

As a neutral country during the war, Mexico was a good place for German spies to covertly enter the United States. To check this threat, undercover U.S. agents in Mexico attempted to stop German agents. In August 1918, the Battle of Ambos Nogales was thought be a product of Berlin's machinations. The Mexican Revolution persisted at Nogales, Sonora, where Villa attacked the *federales*. Villa was defeated, but not before a skirmish with U.S. troops garrisoned at Nogales, Arizona. This time, several Villa rebels and an American were killed. Based on intelligence reports, covert German activities on the border encouraged a battle between the Mexican forces and the U.S. Army. Then the United States learned about a possible attack on Arizona by Mexican soldiers. Prior shootings amplified the tensions between the two countries and erupted into a battle.

U.S. troops successfully ended the border war and possible German military activity in the Southwest. In the aftermath, a chain fence divided the two border towns of Nogales, Sonora, and Nogales, Arizona. Were German advisors on the Mexican side of the border at the Battle of Ambos Nogales? In any case, the hostility between the United States and Germany would have to be fought out in France. Following is the full extent of the Zimmermann Telegram:

> We intend to begin on the first of February unrestricted submarine warfare. We shall endeavor in spite of this to keep the United States of America neutral. In the event of this not succeeding, we make Mexico a proposal of alliance on the following basis: make war together, make peace together, generous financial support and an understanding on our part that Mexico is to reconquer the lost territory in Texas, New Mexico, and Arizona. The settlement in detail is left to you. You will inform the President of the above most secretly as soon as the outbreak of war with the United States of America is certain and add the suggestion that he should, on his own initiative, invite Japan to immediate adherence and at the same time mediate between Japan and ourselves. Please call the President's attention to the fact that the ruthless employment of our submarines now offers the prospect of compelling England in a few months to make peace. Signed, ZIMMERMANN

Chapter 5

Lafayette, We Are Here

June 1917

The year of 1916 ended in despair for the Allies. The planning, execution and control of the offensives on the Western Front had failed to end the war. The French armies were weary. The British suffered unparalleled losses at the Somme without any real gains. Russia was on the threshold of ruin and revolution. The U.S. declaration of war against Germany on April 2, 1917, was an abundant energizer for the Allies, but it would be more than a year before the doughboys would make a difference in the military balance in France. In the new year of 1917, the condition of the armies in Europe was concerning to the commanders. The unease was especially true for the German commanders, who, based on their negative fortunes of war, suffered from high anxiety.

German morale was dazed by the Somme offensive, causing a retreat to the Siegfriedstellung or Hindenburg Line. Constructed twenty-five miles behind the existing front, the Hindenburg Line was in keeping with the "defense in depth" strategy. The heavily fortified line, containing barbed wire and concrete emplacements, required fewer German soldiers, thereby allowing more men to be sent Russia. Nevertheless, Germany's fortunes on the Western Front were not certain. In addition, an Allied blockade continued to effectively limit supplies to the German home front.

In February, the German army retreated to the Hindenburg Line and left a path of destruction with a scorched-earth strategy. In reaction to these factors, German commander Erich Friedrich Wilhelm von Ludendorff resumed the U-boat campaign to stop U.S. supplies from reaching Europe.

General Ludendorff was considered an excellent military strategist; he controlled Germany's war efforts. The Atlantic attacks started while the Germans maintained defensive positions and planned major offensives on the Western Front.

Ludendorff gambled that Germany would win the war before the United States reacted to the unrestricted submarine warfare. He would come to realize that it was a very bad bet. The resumption of attacks on U.S. ships sailing to Allied ports caused President Wilson to break diplomatic relations with Germany. In response to this, New Mexico governor Ezequiel C. de Baca sent the following message to the *New York World*:

New Mexico will stand loyally behind the president and hold up his hands. We endorse the action already taken. We believe the avenues of trade on the high seas should be kept open to commence in accordance with the law of nations and that the armed force of the United States should be used for that purpose if necessary. E.C. de Baca, Governor of New Mexico, Feb. 3, 1917

In April, the British assault at the Battle of Arras gained ground against the Hindenburg defensives. It was the longest one-day gain on the Western Front since the trenches imposed a deadlock, but the battle ended in a stalemate. The British and German casualties totaled almost 250,000. This British offensive was designed to end the war in two days, but the strategy failed. German commanders helped the British by not fully implementing the benefits of their defense in depth. Yet there was no decisive Allied breakthrough, and the offensive cost the British 160,000 soldiers. A good start ended in another bitter disappointment.

President Wilson's long-term policy of maintaining neutrality included loans to Britain and France while maintaining the army at peacetime levels. Predatory German submarine warfare on the Atlantic and the Zimmermann Telegram ended this policy.

With the Atlantic secured and the doughboys trained, the United States was ready to send an army to France. Ironically, the SS *Kaiser Wilhelm II* became an army transport ship. Before the war, the ship was docked in New York. When the United States declared war on Germany, it was confiscated by the federal government and refitted to be a transport ship. With a name change to *Agamemnon*, it regularly steamed across the Atlantic, increasing the U.S. troop numbers to France.

The AEF would ultimately be engaged in the Aisne-Marne, St. Mihiel and Argonne Offensives. The American fighting force was organized in the

1st and 2nd Armies, with the 3rd U.S. Army created at the end of the war. Each army consisted of three corps and five or six divisions.

In June, units of the 1st Infantry Division of the 1st U.S. Army arrived in France. The division's insignia is a big red "1" on a khaki background. The 1st Infantry Division was the first to arrive in France and the first to attack the Germans. Pershing would come to rely on this division for key engagements.

The AEF would fortify the Allies with reinforcements, and when the doughboys arrived in the ports of St. Nazaire, they were wildly welcomed. In a speech by an American general, they heard a rally cry, "Lafayette, we are here." The grand welcome continued when the 1st Infantry Division marched in Paris on the Fourth of July. It was a beginning. A much larger American army was on the way to help the British and the French armies in the Great War.

American soldiers continued to arrive for a period of months. Among the next arriving doughboys were men of the "All-American Division," the nickname of the 82nd Division, which had soldiers from every state. The All-American Division obtained distinction during the final battles of the war. During the Second World War, the division became the first army airborne unit.

In July, a battle occurred for the Belgium city of Ypres without the U.S. army. Although the AEF's arrival increased the morale of the British and the French, the Americans were not ready to join the fight—it was only a matter of time.

The village of Passchendaele was close to Ypres and a German railway junction. Preparations for this Third Battle of Ypres were lacking in clear objectives and a leadership agreement. In November, the long Belgian battle ended with the capture of Passchendaele by Canadian troops. Once again, thousands of lives were lost, with nearly 600,000 casualties for both armies. British troops gained a few miles, with the major mission unaccomplished. Despite this extremely stressful fighting with little success, the British, or at least their leadership, were ready for another offensive. This time, tanks would take a larger role in the assault.

In November, the British Tank Corps launched a large-scale operation against the Hindenburg Line at the Battle of Cambrai. The 325 tanks rolled forward in conjunction with low-flying aircraft striking German positions. At first, the British were successful in penetrating the German lines before a surprise counterattack ended the advance. German antitank defense proved effective in destroying tanks.

Stormtroopers also provided a strong counterpunch. These elite soldiers infiltrated enemy trenches in small units rather than following the earlier massed infantry assaults. Stormtroopers determined the enemy's weak and strong points during an artillery attack, and then when the shelling stopped, they would quickly descend into the trenches. If the stormtroopers broke an Allied line, German infantry would follow up with a continued attack. In the end, there were lessons learned concerning tactical methods of tanks versus trenches, lessons that could end the deadlock.

Victory for the Allies in 1917 continued to be elusive. High losses at Arras and Ypres drove the army's morale down. Some Allied leaders were averse to further risky offensives until the Americans were ready to fight. Over the year, valuable strategic and tactical lessons accrued to the Allied high command. On the other hand, the German army had success with the new stormtrooper assaults, and during the winter, the entrenched army in France was reinforced with divisions redeployed from Russia. The Bolshevik Revolution helped the Germans. At year's end, Russia and Romania ceased fighting with the Central Powers, allowing Germany to transfer thousands of men to the Western Front. This buildup occurred as the Allies faced shortages of men, and the Americans were still months away from entering the fight.

The Yanks were coming. Yet General Pershing would keep the doughboys out of battle until their numbers increased. Beyond numbers, the newly arrived Americans needed three months' training in France. In addition to training his men, General Pershing was engaged in a political fight. The Allied leadership wanted the Americans to become part of French and British units rather than a distinct fighting force. Pershing would keep his doughboys as a national army with American commanders.

As a result, the AEF was sidelined until October 1917, when the newly arrived doughboys occupied positions on the Swiss border and fired their first shots against the Germans. Though on a small scale, the 1st Infantry Division fired the first salvo for the U.S. Army. Then, regiments from the division entered the trenches near Nancy, France. By the end of the year, 130,000 doughboys were in country.

In April 1918, the 2nd U.S. Cavalry arrived in France as the only mounted unit in the AEF. The horse soldiers were on the front lines providing reconnaissance that enhanced aerial scouting. Patrols that located and confirmed German positions were vital to the high command's strategy. In the fall, the mounted men were engaged in the Aisne-Marne Offensive in support of the destruction the Soissons Salient. Also, the 2nd Cavalry played an important role in capturing the St. Mihiel Salient. In the Argonne, 2nd Cavalry troops patrolled and protected the flanks of the attacking U.S. divisions. Along the way, the troopers neutralized a machine gun nests and artillery battery.

By the end of the war, the full force of the AEF, 1.5 million doughboys, were "over there."

Chapter 6

The Western Front

Spring of 1918

In March, *Kaiserschlacht*, an Imperial German battle plan, was launched in Flanders while Germany had the advantage of outnumbering the Allies. This was considered the last best chance to win the war before the Americans arrived. Germany knew the importance of winning in Flanders before the doughboys took the field. The Spring Offensive on the Western Front propelled the Germans almost sixty miles to the west as a preemptive strike before the Americans arrived.

Thousands of German guns and trench mortars opened fire on British positions. Then an infantry assault caused a defensive crisis for the British. Germany's early success was a result of the redeployed troops who became available when Russian surrendered. The German high command believed that the French would seek an armistice—they did not. Instead, General Ferdinand Foch was named general in chief as Allied supreme commander on the Western Front, an attempt toward unity of command. Then the Germans failed to maintain a prolonged mobile operation; their infantrymen were close to exhaustion.

A British counteroffensive convinced the German high command to end the offensive. Although the Germans had advanced, they did not deliver the intended knockout blow. The army moved faster than the supply lines, thereby slowing the advance. By April, it was clear that the Spring Offensive had failed. Of course, the battle increased the loss of men: almost 260,000 casualties for the British and the French combined. Germany suffered 250,000 casualties, including many stormtroopers.

On April 9, Germany started a second scaled offensive, but that drive was stopped. The Allies withstood large losses but were successful in steadying the front lines. At the end of the month, the *Kaiserschlacht* was over and done. The two offensives resulted in more than 330,000 German casualties, a number they especially could not afford given the lack of reserves. Again, Germany's plan failed to be decisive.

During this month, the first tank-versus-tank battle occurred. Tanks were employed before, by the British at the Somme and the French at the Nivelle Offensive. Yet the first tank contest did not occur until late in the war near the village of Villers-Bretonneux. Also, the "Red Baron" was shot down and killed near Amiens; the British buried him with military honors. Manfred von Richthofen, ace German fighter pilot with the *Luftsreitkräfte*, destroyed eighty Allied aircraft in the sky. He was the commander of the *Jagdgeschwader*, or the Flying Circus. The colorful planes and the ground mobility of a traveling circus lead to the colorful name.

Finally, in late April, Ludendorff ended the Flanders offensive. Allied resistance saved the day for France. Germany maintained a strategic edge, despite the two failures. Nevertheless, the massive March and April attacks were turned back by the Allies without the Americans, improving Allied morale.

In the face of U.S. troop reinforcements, Germany's sequence of attacks over the course of the entire spring yielded substantial gains, but the advance was stopped at the Battle of the Aisne. A third German offensive began on May 27 with an attack on the French near the Aisne River. It began with a four-thousand-gun bombardment. German stormtroopers pushed across the river, penetrating Allied lines and arriving within one hundred miles of Paris. Long-range German guns reached Paris and terrorized civilians. The City of Lights was thrown into darkness as citizens evacuated under the cloud of gun smoke and chaos.

The Germans had smashed ahead and by the end of several weeks had reached the Marne near Château-Thierry. Then the doughboys entered the battle. American marines formed positions at Château-Thierry and Belleau Wood and along the Marne. Given the British helmets on the doughboys, the German thought they were English soldiers; they would not make that mistake again. In the Battle of Belleau Wood, the German soldiers allegedly called the marines "Devil Dogs" for their fierce fighting. The Americans fought brilliantly, causing the Germans to realize that taking Paris was a long shot at best. In addition, the U.S. 1st Infantry Division, in reserve of the French army before the attack, captured Cantigny. The first major battle for the doughboys was in the June 1918 Battle of Belleau Wood. French and British forces were also engaged along with the Americans of the 2nd and 3rd Infantry Divisions.

Then an American counterattack with hundreds of Allied tanks stunned the German right flank, stopping the Germans again. The Americans held their ground and showed that they could be trusted to defend Paris. In July, the German army under the command of Ludendorff engaged in a massive assault on the Western Front near the Marne River. It was the last offensive for the German army—the Marne-Reims attack was stopped by the U.S. 2nd Infantry Division.

At the Battle of Soissons, July 11–22, the Germans hoped to win the battle and the war before the Americans arrived in force—or, at least, seek favorable peace terms from the Allies. At first, the Germans had significant gains in capturing territory, soldiers and weapons. Then the Germans slowed down in time enough for the arriving doughboys to reinforce the French and British counterattack. Another offensive gamble was lost to the Germans, along with hundreds of guns and tens of thousands of men. British losses were relatively small. Also, in pushing back the Germans, the French regained their élan.

On August 8, in an effort to remove the Germans from Amiens, the British 4th Army, with 450 tanks, delivered a knockout punch. It was the opening round of the Hundred Days Offensive. This battle of armor ended trench warfare; armies became mobile, foreshadowing the next world war. The scale of defeat at the Battle of Amiens caused many German to surrender and Ludendorff to call that day the "black day of the German army."

Action at Amiens demonstrated improved military leadership, strategy and tactics for the British. Effective use of aircraft, artillery, reconnaissance and the wireless improved battlefield operations. The Amiens victory came when the British army was improving and the German army was declining. Victory meant liberation for French towns, as the German withdrawal continued after the British attack.

After this battle, Germany agreed to a peace conference but maintained a military presence in Flanders for bargaining strength. So, the war continued. On August 29, the French dealt another blow to the Germans, pushing them back a few miles. Later that same month, the British attack caused Ludendorff to surrender much of the gains of the spring and retreat to the Hindenburg Line.

At that point, there was a confidence crisis among many German soldiers, although they remained a tough force. The BEF found resistance from the Alpine Corps as it neared the Hindenburg Line. The Alpine Corps was one of the best divisions in the German army.

In September, the BEF battled its way to positions suited for the final assault. The tide was turning. The Germans were running out of steam, while the British were improving their military leadership and organization and getting better at contingency approaches to battlefield changes. Situational leadership had been learned the hard way in the previous years of war.

The Allied armies defeated General Ludendorff's divisions, exacting a large toll on the German army with 800,000 casualties. The Germans retreated from the Marne and became entrenched, ending the battle and setting the stage for the Second Battle of the Marne. Soon after, General John Pershing and the American 1st Army went into action on September 12 to protect the Paris-Nancy railway with attacks on the occupied St. Mihiel region. Finally, the Allied forces that contained sixteen American divisions and French artillery and tanks defeated the enemy. American troops moved to the Argonne Forest as the Allied armies planned a massive attack against the Germans.

The French and British attacked from the west, and the Americans attacked from the south, a gigantic pincer movement. Weeks of exhausting frontal attacks slowly repelled the Germans, ending with a defeat at the Marne.

With endgame near, the Germans mounted more offensives on the Western Front. However, the Allied counteroffensive, with more than 1 million doughboys, was greater than the German efforts. Then the American army continued to advance against a retreating army that was gasping its last breath. The men of the AEF showed a high spirit of resolve, thereby forcing the enemy to consider ending the war.

The Hundred Days Offensive started on August 8 with a victory at Amiens, France. This was followed by capturing St. Quentin Canal, a German retreat, with the Allies pressing their advantage. On September 29, the British 4th Army launched a twelve-mile attack against the Germans and proceeded with a bombardment of 750,000 shells. The British soldiers penetrated miles into the enemy lines, blasted open a five-mile gap and breached the last defensive line—the Hindenburg Line.

German troops continued to retreat from forward positions. The unstoppable march of the Allied armies convinced the German high command of a grim reality. The unyielding advance ended any remaining optimism, and an armistice became tolerable to the reeling Germans. When Berlin requested peace terms, the Allies insisted that the kaiser abdicate. Reluctantly, Wilhelm II changed the German constitution. A new republic was established in Berlin. The kaiser departed for the Netherlands, and Ludendorff informed Hindenburg that an armistice must be considered.

Chapter 7

American Doughboys

Fall of 1918

The term *doughboy* applied to soldiers and marines who were members of the AEF in World War I. The origin of the name is uncertain. While it was used in the Mexican-American War, it became broadly applied and associated with the men of the AEF. There are several ideas as to the genesis of the term. One possible explanation stems from U.S. soldiers marching in Mexico. The dust that covered the men had a mud brick or adobe color—hence, doughboy.

By the spring of 1918, there were 430,000 American soldiers in France. The Yanks were coming at an increasing rate; by the end of summer, 1 million American fighting men were on the Western Front.

The Americans greatly expanded the Allied army and moved into the front lines at a rate of 250,000 per month. A seemingly endless infusion of doughboys would decrease German resolve, as fears about America's impact were realized. Ultimately, the large U.S. troop movements would be the decisive force in ending the war.

The first major engagement for the United States happened when the American 1st Division countered another German offensive along the Western Front. A regiment of the nearly four thousand men became part of the Aisne-Marne Campaign on May 28, 1918.

A French artillery assault paved the way for a U.S. infantry advance. Then the doughboys advanced into history following French tanks into the German defenses and captured the small town of Cantigny, a German strongpoint and observation position. Since it happened within the larger

Third Battle of Aisne, the importance was reduced. However, it was an American victory and the first test of inexperienced soldiers. The battle showed the world that Americans could stand up to a baptism of fire. Indeed, the Yanks beat battled-hardened German soldiers, proving that they were up to the task.

By late June, the U.S. victory at Cantigny had led to engagements at Château-Thierry and Belleau Wood, where American doughboys were aggressive against the enemy. Army and marine divisions at Château-Thierry stopped the German advance and pushed them across the Marne River. The doughboys held their positions Château-Thierry at the cost of more than ten thousand casualties. Then the American captured Belleau Wood, causing another German retreat.

On July 4, U.S. soldiers joined Australian soldiers at the Battle of Le Hamel in northern France and launched a successful attack against German strong points. The town and the flanking forest was captured. The attack further affected German morale and strategical continued the Allied victories, achieving success in a series of battles.

From July to August, the doughboys were part of the fight against the last German push on the Western Front at the Second Battle of the Marne and the Second Battle of the Somme. At the Marne, French and American divisions stopped the last German offensive of the war. Time was running out. The success at the Second Battle of the Somme accelerated the expiration date for the German army.

In July, the New Mexico National Guard (NMNG) artillery batteries assigned to the U.S. 41st Infantry Division arrived on the Western Front in response to a German offensive. They defended against the enemy at the Marne River, close to Paris. Positions at Château-Thierry, St. Mihiel and the Argonne were maintained by the New Mexico men until the end of the war.

Battery A of the 1st New Mexico Field Artillery became part of the 146th Field Artillery Regiment and the 66th Artillery Brigade within the 41st Division. New Mexico doughboys of this unit achieved great success at Château-Thierry for their role in stopping the last big German offensive. Battery A destroyed the Château-Thierry Bridge and a major German communication channel, an action that contributed to the Allied victory. The guns of the battery fired tens of thousands of rounds—more than the other U.S. artillery units combined.

In addition to the unit Victory Medals, doughboys of Battery A received six battle stars; their commander, Charles M. Debremond, died in 1919 due to the lasting effect of poison gas inhaled in battle. In a letter from General Pershing, Battery A was recognized for highly aggressive action in destroying a key German communication channel: the bridge at Château-Thierry.

When a German attack failed on July 18, the Allies followed up with major counterattack against the Marne, forcing Ludendorff to retreat. In the St. Mihiel assault, New Mexican men of the 143rd and the 144th Machine Battalions manned positions in Roulecourt Forest. Also, Battery A and its 155mm guns saw action at Champagne-Marne, Aisne-Marne and Meuse-Argonne. The doughboy attack on August 6 was against an entrenched German army—it was only a matter of time. In September, the U.S. 1st Army began to penetrate the Argonne Forest as the French advanced on their flank.

The German strategy of the Champagne-Marne offensive, the last one for General Ludendorff, was victory before the Americans arrived in force. It was a race against the clock. They lost several battles, hundreds of thousands of men and the race: the advantage was moved to the Allies.

During the German Spring Offensives, the doughboys provided support for the British and French armies but not as an independent fighting force. That changed in the final epic chapters of the war. General Pershing asserted that his American army would fight the next battles under his command. With a leadership team of Generals George C. Marshall, Douglas MacArthur and Colonel George Patton, that is what happened. The U.S. Army would have a major leadership role in two significant battles that ended the war: St. Mihiel and the Argonne Forest.

ST. MIHIEL

In August 1918, under the leadership of General Pershing, the 1st Army prepared to attack the salient at St. Mihiel, a German strong point that continually resisted previous attacks. The offensive was the sole responsibility of the Americans. At the Battle of St. Mihiel, the American army coined the names "D-Day" and "H-Hour" before the planned attack.

Of course, the salient contained a double line of trenches, barbed wire and pillboxes, and beyond was the formidable Hindenburg Line. This first American-led operation was a grand challenge for the doughboys. The German army would waver from an American army advance—it was the beginning of the end for Germany.

One hour past midnight on September 12, 1918, thousands of French guns roared against the salient. Allied aircraft provided additional support. Doughboys made quick work of the Germans in the first encounter, capturing thousands of men and hundreds of guns. The next job was to capture the land between the river and the forest. American troops advanced over the course of weeks, albeit with seventy-five thousand casualties. An Allied breakthrough happened on September 27: the Hindenburg Line near Cambrai and St. Quentin was breached.

Then the 1st Army, supported by Allied artillery and tanks, launched an attack on the twenty-five-mile-wide strongpoint. If a breakthrough occurred, the plan called for the capture of Metz.

The doughboy attack intended to envelop the salient with a pincer movement, driving the Germans back to the Hindenburg Line; logistical problems with supplies hampered the large-scale operation. Metz was not captured. The Germans entrenched, and the Americans looked to the Argonne Forest.

One important event in the battle was a cavalry-style tank attack under the leadership of Colonel George Patton. The tanks surprised the German infantry, returning the advantage to the doughboys. In the end, America lost seven thousand men. They captured 250 guns and fifteen thousand Germans and reduced the salient. More than two hundred square miles of French territory were recaptured. The Battle of St. Mihiel raised the stature of the U.S. Army with the Allies. This victory was an overture to the last great battle of the war: the Meuse-Argonne.

MEUSE-ARGONNE

The Battle of the Argonne Forest was fought in northeast France, near the Meuse River and the Argonne Forest. It started with a massive bombardment on September 26, 1918, that lasted for six hours. Then, hundreds of Allied tanks ground forward toward the German lines. The infantry was right behind the armored division, supported by the U.S. Air Service. The Meuse-Argonne Offensive, with the Americans taking command, was underway. Many U.S. commanders saw the Argonne, with the strongest German defenses close to supply lines, as the major battle of the war—it would be the final chapter of the war and the endgame for Germany.

With a victory at St. Mihiel, the American leadership quickly moved more than 400,000 men to the Meuse-Argonne. Hundreds of planes bombed German defensive positions and disrupted German reconnaissance. Then the U.S. Army advanced between the Meuse River and the Argonne Forest, a corridor leading to a key German railway.

The U.S. 1st Army and the French 4th Army attacked the German trenches. The opening salvo saw an Allied advance of three miles before the British 1st and 3rd Armies attacked. After an uphill charge in the open, the U.S. 2nd Infantry Division captured the heavily defended high ground of Monfaucon. The division, with an Indian head insignia on a star background, was organized in France at the end of 1917.

This action forced the Germans to retreat from a position that commanded the Champagne region. On October 3, infantry regiments of the Indian Head Division commanded the summit. At the same time, the British were driving in the north to turn the enemy flank, converging with the Americans to contain the Germans.

Eight miles were gained by the end of the month as German resistance hardened. Also, stalemate, attrition and logistical and communication problems stalled the Americans within the German lines, exposing the U.S. leadership to Allied criticism. This led to a temporary cessation of fighting by the Allies. Hence, the U.S. centralized command structure was changed by Pershing, who divided the army into the 1st Army and the new 2nd Army.

Among the soldiers in the Meuse-Argonne Campaign was the highly decorated Sergeant Alvin York of the 82nd Division, who was awarded the Medal of Honor for action in the Argonne. Soldiers of the 308th Infantry, 77th Division (the "Lost Battalion"), were part of the campaign.

Nine companies were isolated by the Germans. Major Charles White Whittlesey and his men advanced, believing that they had flank support. They did not and were surrounded by Germans. These doughboys were faced with shortages of food, water and ammunition and were even bombarded by their U.S. artillery. A homing pigeon, Cher Ami, delivered a crucial message:

WE ARE ALONG THE ROAD PARALLEL 276.4. OUR ARTILLERY IS DROPPING A BARRAGE DIRECTLY ON US. FOR HEAVENS SAKE STOP IT

Also, on October 3, Germany and Austria sent peace messages to the United States, with Germany determined to keep eastern territories they believed to be German. On October 5, the last Hindenburg defense was broken. Ludendorff's message to Berlin that the war was lost shocked the politicians. American and French soldiers continued to force the Germans to retreat; the British and Belgians did the same in northern Flanders.

By early October, the Germans were forced into a general retreat along fifty miles of the Western Front; the American and French forces continued to advance. By mid-October, the Germans were retreating along the Belgian coast and northeast France. The Belgian and British forces continued to advance.

Now German troop strength was weak, but they were still able to slow down the Allied juggernaut. By October 19, the Allies were close to the Dutch frontier. This was the last battle, as a German defeat seemed inevitable. Then, on October 23, the Allies sought an unconditional surrender.

After steady resistance to attacks for weeks, the Allies were able to break through the German lines. The advancing Allies found thousands of German soldiers willing to surrender. In the face of heavy casualties, the doughboys smashed the German defenses.

On November 1, the Allied armies briefly stopped the juggernaut to regroup, and then the doughboys continued advancing with attacks on German positons near the Meuse River. The Belgian and British armies moved closer to Belgium, while the U.S. 1st Army captured the last major German defensive line and soon after held the important Lille-Metz Railroad. For the Central Powers, the curtain was coming down.

Over the course of weeks of frontal assaults, the Germans were pushed back until late November 1, when the Argonne Forest was free of the invading army. At last, the Allies forced the Germans out of the Argonne. The Germans suffered 100,000 casualties; the Americans recorded 117,000 casualties. It was a high-price victory, but it would end the war.

In Berlin, the leadership was informed that the German army was exhausted and could not win the war. The Germans responded by reinforcing the Argonne front for a better negotiating positon in the coming armistice, showing no signs of surrender.

Doughboys of the 1st and 2nd Armies continued to attack German positions near the Meuse River. Also, U.S. army reinforcements advanced twenty miles before the armistice. At the same time, Allies continued to advance in Belgium. Subsequently, a republic was declared in Berlin, paving the way for a German party to cross no man's land to meet the French commander. With defeat certain, Germany requested a peace agreement.

On November 5, President Wilson told the Germans that peace discussions could begin with French field marshal Ferdinand Foch. According to the terms, Germany had to leave all occupied lands and submit to an Allied occupation west of the Rhine River. The armistice was signed in the railroad car of Field Marshal Foch, the Allied supreme commander, in Compiègne, France. The war ended on November 11, 1918.

Chapter 8

New Mexico Doughboys I

In 1852, New Mexico had nine counties. Before the First World War, Santa Ana County was annexed to Bernalillo County; after the war, Los Alamos was created from parts of Sandoval and Santa Fe Counties. In 1918, Cibola was created from the western part of Valencia County; in 1921, Harding was created from parts of Mora and Union Counties. Doughboys, presented alphabetically by county, represent the 11,690 New Mexicans who served in the war.

Soldier stories in this section address Bernalillo, Catron, Chaves, Cibola, Colfax, Curry, De Baca and Dona Ana Counties. The corresponding county seats are Albuquerque, Reserve, Roswell, Grants, Raton, Clovis, Fort Sumner and Las Cruces.

★★★

Rafael Pargas, from Albuquerque in Bernalillo County, was on patrol with Company I, 356th Infantry, 89th Division, on the Western Front. It was August 18, 1918, at 2100 hours. It was not a walk in the French countryside; German fire opened up and surprised the company. The damage of that attack was limited to several men, who had their uniforms torn up by wire entanglements. At dawn, the patrol made its way back to the American lines.

Later, Pargas and his company moved via railway to Hannonville-sous-les-Côtes, closer to the Meuse-Argonne region. The company was outfitted with

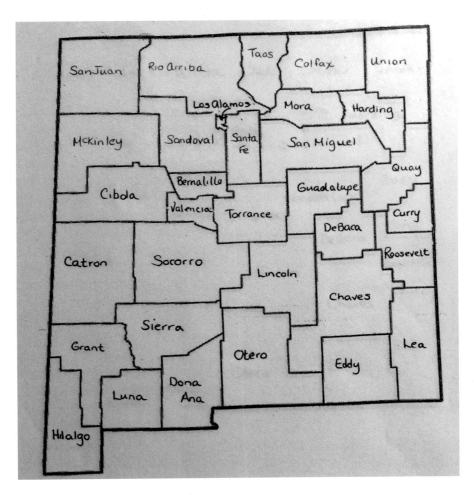

New Mexico county map. Author's collection.

"over the top" equipment, prepared to engage in the Battle of the Argonne Forest. It was the last Allied campaign and ended with the armistice.

On September 11, 1918, Pargas and his company waited in trenches that were so filled with mud that the men stood up all night. In the morning, the companies in the battalion advanced, attacked and captured two hundred German soldiers. Company I remained engaged in its sector until the night of November 10, 1918. Then the battalion crossed the Meuse River and continued to advance.

At daybreak, a German machine gun nest was observed on the right of the battalion on the last day of the war. Pargas and his company moved out to silence the machine guns, and the guns were silenced. The men killed or drove away the enemy and captured five machine guns and a big field gun. It came with a cost: three men in the company were killed, including the company's last officer, reducing the company strength to forty-seven men.

On that morning of November 11, 1918, just hours before the armistice was signed, Company I was dug in along a stone road and, as Pargas wrote, "taking every preparation against treachery on the part of the Germans."

After the armistice, the 89th Division marched from France to Germany as part of the Army of Occupation. The divisions that entered Germany, Austria and Hungary remained in Europe until 1923. Doughboy Pargas was stationed in Germany until in June 1919, when he returned to the United States and to New Mexico.

Rafael Pargas.

FRANK ALARID of Albuquerque stopped at Camp Mills on the way to France. The camp was a temporary tent city embarkation point for soldiers, located ten miles east of New York in Long Island. From Hoboken, New Jersey, he sailed on a twelve-day journey to Liverpool, England, finally arriving in Camp Cherbourg in France on June 28, 1918.

On August 5, Alarid was positioned with Company F, 314th Engineers, 89th Division, in the Toul Sector of the battlefield. At the front, near a bulge in the lines, the St. Mihiel Salient, he became part of a successful assault

Frank Alarid.

against the German defenses. In October, the Allies continued to press their advantage to the Meuse-Argonne woods, the last big offensive of the war. Alarid was engaged at the Battle of the Argonne Forest until November 11, 1918.

After the armistice, his regiment stayed in the Argonne Forest for two weeks before marching through Belgium and Luxembourg, arriving in Germany in December, where Doughboy Alarid remained until May 1919.

CRECENSIO MATA was from Alameda in Bernalillo County—a county, with the most population in the state, that contains the Cibola National Forest. He enlisted in the army at Albuquerque in June 1918.

During the Mexican Revolution, General Pershing organized border security at Fort Bliss in El Paso, Texas. As a result, Fort Bliss became a major base that contributed to the war effort as an enlistment center, training center and mobilization point for soldiers going to France, including doughboy Mata. From Fort Bliss, he was assigned to Camp Jackson, South Carolina, and moved to Newport Beach, Virginia.

In September 1918, he sailed to Brest, France, an embarkation port for men on the way to the Western Front. The U.S. Navy maintained an air

station for seaplanes at Brest as well. In October, from Bordeaux, Mata was assigned to Battery E, 124th Field Artillery, 58th Brigade, 33rd Division, and was engaged at Brocourt Wood, twenty miles west of Amiens in northern France. Battery E moved to the firing line and secured positions at Romange.

At the Battle of the Meuse-Argonne, doughboy Mata and his 58th Brigade of Artillery provided support for the 89th Division. The brigade continued bombarding German positions right up to Armistice Day. After the Allied victory, Mata marched to Luxembourg as part of the Army of Occupation and stayed until returning to the United States in June 1919.

Crecensio Mata.

CARL BROREIN from Albuquerque was a University of New Mexico graduate and a Marine Corps captain. He was assigned to the 1st Marine Aeronautic Company, stationed in Pont Delgada, Azores, the volcanic islands about nine hundred miles west of Portugal.

In January 1918, the Marine Corps established an air station at the American Naval Base in the Azores. It was the first full-service American aviation unit to be completely established and trained in the war zone. As part of that service, Captain Brorein trained other pilots who gave air support for ground forces on the Western Front.

On the North Atlantic, the aviation company went into action in anti-submarine warfare around the British coast. Over the sea, aero squadrons flew U-boat patrols, bombed submarines bases and escorted vessels. Over the land, aero planes helped Allied infantry with tactical bombing of Germany defenses and by shooting down enemy reconnaissance balloons. Captain Brorein was honorably discharged from service in August 1919.

Carl Brorein.

FIDEL BACA of Tijeras in Bernalillo County was a farmer before becoming a solider. He trained in Camp Funston, Kansas. The training camp was established at Fort Riley, Kansas, for men from Midwest states and from Arizona, Colorado and New Mexico.

He moved to Camp Kearny, California, one of the many new camps where thousands of men passed through before receiving orders for assignments. From there, he was sent to Camp Merritt in Hoboken, New Jersey, and boarded a ship for France.

As an infantryman, doughboy Baca served on the battlefields on the Western Front for the last six months of the war in the fall of 1918. During that time, he engaged the enemy and contributed to the final knockout

Fidel Baca.

Vincente Baneras.

blows against the German army that ended the war. While fighting to defeat the kaiser's army, Baca suffered three combat wounds. He was honorably discharged in June 1919 and returned to New Mexico and to farming.

VINCENTE BANERAS, a farmer and cowboy before becoming a soldier, was from the town of Reserve in Catron County. Reserve was the scene of lawyer and lawman Elfego Baca's "Frisco Shootout" in 1884. Catron, located in the southwestern part on New Mexico, is the largest county in the state in terms of territory.

When doughboy Baneras, of Company B, 20th Infantry, was about to join the fight in France, the Spanish influenza quarantined his unit for two months. The influenza pandemic was another disaster of massive proportions. A war that killed millions in battle ended in a haunting time of death by disease. The worldwide death toll from the "Spanish flu" is estimated to be as high as 100 million in 1918–19. In the fall of 1918, almost 700,000 Americans died from influenza in the United States. In New Mexico, some 15,000 people became sick and more than 1,000 died. In the army, half of the U.S. soldiers who died in France were victims of the Spanish flu rather than German bullets—some 57,000 soldiers succumbed to the virus. When the quarantine ended, doughboy Baneras and his unit were ready to go "over there." Then, Armistice Day ended the war.

EUSTACE T. BOYER was from Blackdom in Chaves County, located in the southeastern part of New Mexico. In 1903, a town was founded by Francis Marion Boyer as a black frontier town near Roswell, New Mexico. Within a few years, the Blackdom Townsite Company

Eustace T. Boyer.

was thriving economically and was a site of oil exploration that created the Blackdom Oil Company. Due to the Great Depression, Blackdom became a ghost town. The Dust Bowl claimed the town but not its history.

Doughboy Boyer arrived at Brest, France, in January 1918 with the 351st Machine Gun Battalion, 92nd Division. From there, he was assigned to the St. Die Sector in the Champagne region in the northeast of France. Pershing's operational plan divided the battlefield into several sectors by corps. Each corps maneuvered within assigned boundaries. By September, he was at the front in the Argonne Forest. In October 1918, he wrote a letter to his mother, including, in part:

Dear Mother, I thought I would drop you a few lines while sitting here and thinking of you and home. This letter leaves me well and I hope when these few lines reach your loving hands it will find you well and engaged in the best of life….from your loving son

Pvt. Eustace T. Boyer, Co, D 351 M.G. Bn. American E.F.

CORPORAL DAVID REAVIS of Roswell in Chaves County was a rancher before becoming a motorcycle dispatch rider in the army. He was sent to Camp Funston and then to Camp Mills before arriving in Le Havre, France. As a dispatch rider heading to the front, Reavis had opportunities to see much of the war in the face of German fire and extremely rough terrain. Delivering messages was a vital job: leadership takes action through the communication process.

Although often times more immediate communication was needed, commanders relied on motorcycle couriers to direct battle plans. The size and weight of radios of the day rendered them impractical in the battlefield. For action as a dispatch rider in the St. Mihiel and Meuse-Argonne Offensives,

David Reavis.

doughboy Reavis received a citation from General Pershing and the *Croix de Guerre* (Cross of War) from the French. During the war, the *Croix de Guerre* was given to Allied soldiers, including some American doughboys.

FLOYD H. WELLS of Roswell in Chaves County was drafted in May 1918 and sent to Camp Dodge, Iowa; Camp Gordon, Georgia; and Camp Upton, Long Island, New York, before sailing to Liverpool, England. From Southampton, England, he embarked to Le Havre, France. Within days, Wells and the 82nd Division arrived at the British reserve near the mouth of the Somme River. In June, the division left the British sector for the American sector and entered the trenches.

On October 16, 1918, Wells and his squad were holding an outpost ahead of the front lines in the Argonne Forest. One of the men was shot. Wells and another soldier carried the wounded man back to the American line under machine gun and artillery fire. Wells was awarded the Distinguished Service Cross from General Pershing and the *Croix de Guerre* from Marshall Petain. In the image here, doughboy Wells is pictured standing to the right with two friends, wearing his two medals on his uniform.

AMADO GARCIA was from Acomita in what is now Cibola County in the western part of New Mexico. Acomita is part of Acoma Pueblo in western New Mexico, about sixty miles from Albuquerque. The Acoma people have lived in the region for more than eight hundred years.

In June 1918, doughboy Garcia enlisted in the army and was assigned to Company K, 110th Infantry, 28th Division. Two months later, he was near the small town of Fismes, France, in the Champagne region. At the beginning of the battle, some two thousand U.S. soldiers were killed trying to cross the Vesle River and capture Fismes. In the end, the town was almost completely destroyed.

During this turmoil, Garcia and two other men advanced hundreds of yards into no man's land and through barbed wire to attack a German machine gun position. Despite a fury of fire, the U.S. soldiers killed some of the crew and caused the rest to flee. They captured the machine gun and returned to their regiment's lines under heavy fire. For his drive, Garcia was cited for bravery and awarded the **Distinguished Service Cross** for action in the face of mortal danger. **Garcia returned to New Mexico and served as lieutenant governor of Acoma Pueblo.**

Floyd H. Wells (*far right*), with doughboys.

DOROTEO LOPEZ of Colfax County, located in northeastern New Mexico on the Colorado border, was a farmer before entering the service. In October 1917, he was assigned to Camp Funston and then to Camp Kearny. From Camp Merritt in New Jersey, he sailed to France in June 1918 and joined Company C, 110th Infantry, 28th Division.

Doroteo Lopez.

Once in France, doughboy Lopez was on the front lines with the 110th Infantry and faced the last major German offensive of the war. Then Lopez and his unit were part of the advance on the Vesle River near the city of Reims. Finally, the division was engaged at the Thiaucourt Sector of the Meuse-Argonne Campaign and remained there on the front lines until Armistice Day. In April 1919, Lopez sailed back across the Atlantic and arrived in Philadelphia in May 1919— "to the good USA," as he wrote.

LIEUTENANT LEO HENRY DAWSON of Colfax County and the U.S. Army Air Service was a command pilot and combat observer in France. He ascended in the air and in the ranks. As a member of the 94th Aero Squadron, he shot down four German airplanes. He received the Distinguished Service Cross, "awarded for actions during the World War I," as detailed here in the War Department General Orders No. 21 (1919):

The President of the United States of America, authorized by Act of Congress, July 9, 1918, takes pleasure in presenting the Distinguished Service Cross to First Lieutenant (Air Service) Leo H. Dawson, United States Army Air Service, for extraordinary heroism in action while serving with 94th Aero Squadron, 1st Pursuit Group, U.S. Army Air Service, A.E.F., near Hartennes, France, 19 July 1918. While on a voluntary patrol, Lieutenant Dawson encountered seven enemy monoplanes at an altitude of 2,000 meters. After a brief engagement his guns jammed, but, after repairing the jam in the air, and under heavy fire, he returned to the fight, shot down one of the enemy in flames and drove off the others.

Lieutenant Dawson also received a Bronze Oak Leaf for attacking four German aero planes, as detailed here in the War Department General Orders No. 21 (1919):

> *The President of the United States of America, authorized by Act of Congress, July 9, 1918, takes pleasure in presenting a Bronze Oak Leaf Cluster in lieu of a Second Award of the Distinguished Service Cross to First Lieutenant (Air Service) Leo H. Dawson, United States Army Air Service, for extraordinary heroism in action while serving with 94th Aero Squadron, 1st Pursuit Group, U.S. Army Air Service, A.E.F., near Clery-le-Petit, France, 4 November 1918. Sighting four enemy planes (type Rumpler), Lieutenant Dawson immediately attacked, despite the numerical superiority of the enemy, and destroyed one of the group, whereupon the remaining three scattered and returned to their lines.*

In addition to his World War I aerial exploits, Dawson became a colonel in World War II and witnessed history at the end of the war. Colonel Dawson was on board the USS *Missouri* for the formal surrender of Japan on September 2, 1945.

Edward Springer.

CAPTAIN EDWARD T. SPRINGER of Colfax County was assigned to the 21st Field Artillery, 5th Division, which arrived in France in May 1918. As reported in the *Las Vegas Daily Optic*, "Fifth Division Does Gallant Fighting, Capt. Springer, Local Boy, in Thick of Fray for 27 days."

On September 12, the 5th Division was deployed in the major attacks at St. Mihiel and the Meuse-Argonne that ended the war. A Las Vegas newspaper went on to say that the division "was hotly engaged under shell, rifle and machine gun fire for 27 of the last 30 days of the war." An official citation from the division commander was issued on November 11, 1918, reading, in part:

> *This is a brilliant example of what American soldiers can do in an emergency when he must go on to the utmost of his power. The Division commander is proud of the work of the Division. No Division could have*

accomplished more and every member of the command should be proud to belong to a division which so brilliantly ended its record in the greatest war the world as know.

H.E. Ely
Major General, U.S.A. Commanding

LAURIANO MARTINEZ was from the ranching community of Colmor in Colfax County, near the Great Plains and the Rocky Mountains. Today, Colmar is a ghost town. In August 1918, doughboy Martinez, Company K, 110th Infantry, 28th Division, was engaged in battle at Fismes, France. The Battle of Fismes and the nearby town of Fismette foreshadowed the street fighting that was common in World War II after Normandy.

Along with two others soldiers, Martinez crawled three hundred yards over no man's land through barbed wire and attacked a German machine gun nest. Despite facing fire at close range, the doughboys drove out the enemy with clubbed rifles and returned to the American lines under continued fire. For this extraordinary bravery in action, Martinez was awarded the Distinguished Service Cross.

CORPORAL PATRICK CHAVEZ was from the coal mining town of Van Houten, New Mexico, Colfax County. During the war, the town's Red Cross chapter sold more than $100,000 in Liberty War Bonds.

Corporal Chavez arrived in Le Havre, France, in July 1918. At Camp De Souge, he attended artillery training on the French 75mm rapid-firing artillery piece. Field artillery batteries increased in importance on the Western Front as a vital part of strategies and tactics. The improved weapons had greater range, limiting safe area for the infantry. A barrage before an infantry attack would confuse the defending soldiers.

In September, his unit, Battery A, 341st Field Artillery, 89th Division, left for the front to positions in the Toul Sector and then to the recently reduced salient at St. Mihiel. Chavez and his regiment participated in the first raid on Bois Dommertin and then supported the infantry in a general raid of the sector. The 341st Field Artillery stayed in action and continued to confuse the Germans until Armistice Day.

CORPORAL GEORGE WILLIAM BROWNELL of Curry County, located in eastern New Mexico on the Texas border, was an original member of the 186th Aero Squadron. In November 1917, the squadron started a flying

George Brownell.

Frank Culberson.

school at Kelly Field, Texas. Two months later, the trained squadron transferred to the Aviation Concentration Center at Camp Mills. Then the squadron prepared for the transatlantic crossing.

Doughboy Brownell and the 186th sailed to England on the White Star Line ship RMS *Adriatic*. The upscale passenger ocean liner served as a troop transfer ship and carried the squadron to Liverpool, England, where they crossed the channel.

In August 1918, the unit arrived in Le Havre, France, and at the St. Maixent Aerodrome for processing. Ultimately, the group was assigned to the 1st Army Observation group and performed strategic reconnaissance of the German positions on the Western Front. Brownell and the squadron participated in the Meuse-Argonne Offensives with reconnaissance of Germany territory and information gathering.

LIEUTENANT FRANK MORGAN CULBERSON was from De Baca County. The county is located in the eastern part of New Mexico and named for Governor Ezequiel Cabeza de Baca. Before the army, Culberson attended the New Mexico Normal University and was a high school principal at Farmington High School and at Portales High School.

In October 1918, he was with the 6th Infantry Division near the Meuse River. The division conducted patrols in no man's land and behind the German lines. Lieutenant Culberson's company, positioned in front of enemy batteries, received "showers of shrapnel at various intervals." Culberson, wounded in the knee by shrapnel, was forced to the first-aid station. The night sky was filled with fast action: German planes raided Allied lines, and the Allies returned the favor.

On November 4, Culberson and the 3rd Battalion moved to Brueilles, built bridges and crossed the river under heavy fire. They reached the heights and captured many German soldiers. The battalion received a citation from the commanding general for its success. Days before the armistice, Culberson was made Company K commander and took charge of an outpost. On Armistice Day, the 6th Infantry advanced on the French towns of Jametz and Remoirville, one of the last actions of the war.

On December 1, as part of the Army of Occupation, Culberson and his unit started toward the German town of Trier, located on the banks of the Moselle River. The men crossed the river—which flows though France, Luxembourg and Germany—and took over a German barracks in Trier. On July 4, 1919, the unit sailed to the United States. Culberson returned to New Mexico and became a teacher and a rancher.

CORPORAL RICARDO APODACA of Las Cruces in Dona Ana County, located in southern New Mexico on the Texan and Mexican borders, prepared for embarkation at Camp Wheeler in Macon, Georgia. He was assigned to a Signal Corps unit, Company C, 105th Field Signal Battalion, 31st Division.

He was transferred to Camp Mills before sailing to France. On October 7, 1918, the division set sail on the British ship *Euripides*. Two weeks later, the ship arrived in Brest, France, an important Brittany harbor city. There, he joined the Signal Corps Replacement area at Cour-Cheverny in central France and was garrisoned at a village of Bracieux.

Ricardo Apodaca.

Apodaca and the Army Signal Corps supported the vital command and control functions of the AEF and its infantry divisions on the Western Front. In the spring after the armistice, he moved to a point of embarkation at Bordeaux. Doughboy Apodaca returned to the United States and Camp Upton in Long Island, the last stop before his discharge in Fort Bliss, Texas.

LAURENS WEAVER WEDDELL, from Las Cruces, in Dona Ana County, was a college graduate and journalist before becoming a soldier. He attended officer training camp at Leon Springs, Texas, and was commissioned a first lieutenant, infantry. Lieutenant Weddell was ordered to France immediately. From Le Havre, he was sent to Valréas for infantry officer's school, trench warfare instruction and machine gun school.

In November 1917, he was assigned to Company B, 5th Machine Gun Battalion, 23rd Infantry, 2nd Division, and was positioned near Bourmont on the Meuse River. Over the hard winter of 1917–18, Lieutenant Weddell and his men built barracks, bridges and roads.

Laurens Weddell.

As the season changed, so did his location; between March and May, he held positions in the trenches in southwest of Verdun. Lieutenant Weddell engaged in trench raids and small attacks. The next mission involved a fifty-mile hike to Château-Thierry with Weddell as company commander. On June 2, Company B "came into contact with the Hun." For more than a month, his unit remained in "active desperate contact" until relieved.

The relief was short-lived, as the men took motor trucks to Soissons to be part of Allied supreme commander Ferdinand Foch's July offensive. Two U.S. divisions, under French command, supported twenty-four French divisions. Along with almost five hundred tanks, the French and Americans recaptured lost territory. Lieutenant Weddell was cited in General Orders for bravery in action. His next mission was in Nancy, France, where his unit assumed positions at the Pont a Mousson Sector. In August, he was assigned to 1st Corps Schools as a machine gun instructor at Gondrecourt until the end of the war. He was promoted to captain in January 1919.

Captain Weddell reflected on his war experience in his own words: "America accomplished wonders in the war. She performed the impossible and overcame seemingly insurmountable barriers."

YSABEL GRANILLO descended from the Tiguas Indians of Isleta Pueblo, located south of Albuquerque in the Rio Grande Valley in what is now Cibola County. Founded in the fourteenth century, Isleta has the Manzano Mountains to the east and high desert lands to the west.

In the mid-1870s, doughboy Granillo's father served in the U.S. Army as a Pueblo Indian scout. Granillo, of Las Cruces, served with the 109th Infantry, 28th Division. In June 1918, he sailed for France and participated in the Battle of Château-Thierry, where the Germans breached Allied lines and the Americans stopped the advance before Paris was captured.

On August 14, 1918, Granillo was gassed in battle and sent to the hospital. After his recovery, he was back on the front lines. This time, he was engaged at the St. Mihiel drive at the Verdun Front. As was the case for thousands of soldiers, he was stricken with influenza and sent to a field hospital. The war was over for Ysabel Granillo.

Ysabel Granillo.

UIL LANE was a science teacher at La Cruces High School (1915–16) before entering the army. Doughboy Lane served as a sergeant at the Mexican border with the 1st New Mexico Infantry from May 1916 until his discharge in January 1917.

In May 1917, he attended ROTC and became a second lieutenant, soon to be off to France. Lieutenant Lane participated in action at the September and October offensives at St. Mihiel and Meuse-Argonne with the 361st Infantry Regiment, 91st Division. Then he was engaged at the Lys Schelt Offensive in Belgium, near the Schelt River and the town of Audeuande.

Uil Lane.

On November 2, Lieutenant Lane was wounded at Audeuande and remained incapacitated for six weeks. In that Belgian town, a World War I

American Monument has an inscription that reads, "Erected by the United States of America to commemorate the service of the American troops who fought in this vicinity October 30–November 11, 1918."

Americans killed in this offensive are buried in the Flanders Field American Cemetery in Waregem, Belgium. In April 1919, Lieutenant Lane and the 361st Infantry regiment demobilized at Camp Lewis, Washington.

Soldier stories in this section address Eddy, Grant, Guadalupe, Hidalgo, Lea, Lincoln and Luna Counties. The corresponding county seats are Carlsbad, Silver City, Santa Rosa, Lordsburg, Lovington, Carrizozo and Deming.

LIEUTENANT AUD EDWARD LUSK from Carlsbad in Eddy County, in southern New Mexico at Texas state line, attended the New Mexico Military Institute. After officer training at Camp Logan in Houston, Texas, he was sent to Camp Upton for embarkation to France.

Lieutenant Lusk and the 33rd Division landed in Brest, France, and rushed north to Picardy with units of the British army in defense of Amiens. It was August 8, 1918. The battle ended trench warfare as armies resumed mobile tactics and started the battles that lead to the armistice. Then Lusk and the division were part of the British counteroffensive on the Somme until August 24.

Aud Edward Lusk.

On September 8, the unit entrained and headed for the front, where it was outfitted with American equipment and assigned to the U.S. 1st Army. Its position was at Hill 304—"Dead Man's Hill." Located near the Meuse River at Verdun, Hill 304 was a maelstrom of many fierce fights in the last two years of the war.

As part of the 1st Army, the 33rd Division attacked the German lines in the Battle of the Meuse-Argonne. The men crossed the Meuse River under heavy fire and reached their objective on time. After being relieved by

French colonials, Lusk's division headed for the rear for replacements and new equipment.

On November 10, the division was back on the front line, this time as part of the 2nd Army, and launched an attack on Metz. The attack ended the next day, Armistice Day. After the war, doughboy Lusk remained in Luxembourg with the Army of Occupation. In March 1919, he sailed back to the United States and then traveled overland by rail to New Mexico.

CAPTAIN WILLIAM DEAN of Carlsbad—near the Pecos River, the Guadalupe Mountains and the Carlsbad Caverns—served as a private during the Spanish-American War in Cuba. Both of his grandfathers served the Confederacy during the Civil War. In 1909, he enlisted in the New Mexico National Guard as a sergeant and ascended through the ranks to captain. In 1913, he was the commander of Company B, 1st New Mexico Infantry. Captain Dean answered the president's call and served on the Mexican border from May 1916 to April 1917 in Columbus and Hachita, New Mexico.

One night in June 1916, he was ordered by Colonel Charles Farnsworth to enter Mexico with twenty men. The mission was to warn an outpost of U.S. soldiers that two thousand armed Mexicans were near their position. Dean's command and all the men in the outpost safely returned to Columbus. Colonel Farnsworth, as a major general, went on to command the 37th Division in France.

In April 1917, Dean answered the president's call to serve again, this time in the Great War. He was assigned to command Company B, 143rd Machine Gun Battalion, 40th Division, and remained as company commander throughout the war. In August 1918, he arrived in France. While at Gondrecourt, the roar and flashes of the guns from St. Mihiel were apparent. Then Company B was located close to the aerial bombardments at Nancy, France.

In October, Dean's company, along with the battalion, was ordered to Amiens in northern France for the start of the Hundred Days Offensive. After the Allied victory at Amiens, Dean and his company remained in that position until November 11, 1918.

SECOND LIEUTENANT BRYAN MUDGETT of Eddy County was in action with the 357th Infantry Division at St. Mihiel. During the September 12 advance, Lieutenant Mudgett and his men outflanked enemy machine gun nests and captured the guns and the German crews.

William Dean.

In addition, he led a patrol into the German line and captured a battery manned by a noncommissioned officer and seven men. Through German fire, he led his men back to the U.S. lines, meeting the advancing Americans on the way. For this action, doughboy Mudgett was awarded the Distinguished Service Cross.

In 1913, OBART HARTSHORN of Eddy County enlisted in Company B, 1st New Mexico Infantry, and served on the Mexican border in 1916. Then he attended officer training camp at the Presidio in San Francisco. In 1776, the Spanish founded the outpost for its lands in the North American West. After Mexico won independence from Spain, the Presidio came under Mexican control until the United States won the Mexican-American War in 1847.

In 1917, Hartshorn was commissioned a second lieutenant of infantry and assigned to the 91st Division at Camp Lewis, Washington. Lieutenant Hartshorn arrived in France with the 35th Division in April 1918. During the St. Mihiel drive, his unit was in reserve for the Meuse-Argonne drive. While platoon leader of the 130th Machine Gun Battalion, he was shot and evacuated to Base Hospital 14 in Bordeaux.

A promotion to first lieutenant followed his hospital time. He rejoined the 130th Machine Gun Battalion for the St. Mihiel drive near Metz. When the war ended, he transferred to the 5th Division of the Army of Occupation in Luxembourg. In July 1919, he returned home on the USS *America*. Lieutenant Hartshorn reflected on the war in his own words:

> *I think the war terminated about one month too soon because if the war had gone on that much longer there is no doubt but that we should have had an annihilated Germany instead of one that claims that she was whipped in*

Obart Hartshorn.

an economic way instead of a military way. It would have had a far greater moral effect upon the rising generations of Germans and we would not have had the trouble over carrying out the terms of the artistic and eventually the terms of peace.

I think that the result of the war is disappointing, that the only benefit derived form it is the fact that the world is temporarily free from the Teutonic menace and that it brought home to us the fact that must have a fairly large army and navy and above all things a <u>disciplined</u> one. I believe that the future peace of the world depends on the future development of Russia. If the Allies do not develop Russia the Allies will and a combination of Germany, Russia and Japan will be a far greater menace than the Old Triple Alliance was.

EARL SPRAGUE BULLOCK of Silver City in Grant County was a student at the time he enlisted in August 1917. Grant County, named for the former president, is located in the southwestern part of New Mexico on the Arizona border.

Bullock's grandfathers were Civil War soldiers: Silas Bullock was a sergeant with the 8th Michigan Cavalry, and T.F. Rodenbough, a 2nd U.S. Cavalry officer, received the Congressional Medal of Honor with this citation: "Handled the regiment with great skill and valor, was severely wounded." His great-grandfather was a U.S. admiral in the War of 1812. Other ancestors were soldiers in the American Revolution. Bullock joined Ambulance Company 3 at Fort Bliss,

Earl Sprague Bullock.

Texas. In October 1917, the company went to Vicksburg, Mississippi, to attend to the sick at a Civil War veterans' reunion.

Ambulance Company 3 sailed for France, arriving in December 1917 to join the 1st Sanitary Train, 1st Division. As part of the Medical Department, the company was charged with carrying wounded men from the battlefield to the dressing stations and field hospitals. On January 30, 1918, Bullock saw action at the Ansauville Sector. Then he was in the Battle of Cantigny, the Aisne-Marne and the Second Battle of the Marne. Finally, at the St. Mihiel and Argonne Offensive, he was cited in General Orders for evacuating wounded under heavy fire.

After the armistice, he marched into Germany with his unit as part of the Army of Occupation. Doughboy Bullock stayed in the defeated country until January 1919, when a tuberculosis diagnosis him sent back to the United States and New Mexico.

Some eighty thousand French soldiers were sent home with tuberculosis in 1916, and French citizens were quickly becoming victims of the disease. In the United States, Americans were painfully aware of tuberculosis reaching alarming proportions. The British army had high rates of the disease as well. The American Red Cross created a Commission for the Prevention of Tuberculosis to help the doughboys as much as possible.

IVORY H. CHAPIN, from the town of Hurley in Grant County, was part of the Army Medical Department in 1918. In France, he was with the 101st Ambulance Company, 101st Sanitary Train, 26th Division. Back in 1775, the Continental Congress had created the Army Medical Department and Hospital Department for the U.S. Army.

Given the great rate of casualties, there was a great need for medical support systems. As a result, the Army Medical Department experienced a major expansion during the war. At the start of the war, there were about 1,000 soldiers in the department; at the end of the war, there were 350,000 soldiers, including doughboy Chapin, who was a recipient of the Distinguished Service Cross, "awarded for actions during the World War I":

> *The Distinguished Service Cross is presented to Ivory H. Chapin, Private, U.S. Army, for extraordinary heroism in action at Wadonville, France, September 25, 1918. Private Chapin assisted in establishing a dressing station in a dugout under heavy shell fire. When it was destroyed by a shell he worked unceasingly in the open under fire from enemy machine guns and snipers, caring for the wounded. He remained at his post for several hours after his station had been ordered closed, permitting neither his own exhaustion nor the enemy fire to deter him from aiding the wounded.*

WILLIAM HARBIN's grandfather Jesse Washington Harbin served in the war against Old Mexico and in the Civil War. Doughboy Harbin of Cuerro in Guadalupe County served in many World War I battles. He was assigned to Truck Train 24 and then to Company D, 2nd Supply Train.

William Harbin.

Supplying 2 million U.S. soldiers in France was a great challenge. Huge amounts of ammunition, food and medical and other supplies had to be transported at unprecedented levels on a daily basis—and through roads that were often is disrepair and at times under attack.

Harbin arrived and remained at the Verdun Front from March through May 1918. He was transferred to the Château-Thierry, to Soissons and then to Metz. In the final months of the war, he served in the last big offensives at St. Mihiel and the Meuse-Argonne.

With Germany defeated, he became part of the Army of Occupation until April 1919. Harbin arrived in the United States wearing three Gold Army Service chevrons on the lower sleeves of his uniform, indicating his combat service.

JOHN BROCKMAN, from the town of Mills in Mora County (Harding County in 1921), was assigned to Company A, 113th Mounted Machine Gun Battalion, 30th Division. In June 1918, Brockman and the division landed in France to be assigned to the British army on the Somme Sector. He was engaged in several key battles, including at Ypres, St. Quintin Canal and Mazinghem.

In September 1918, the Battle of St. Quentin Canal began, becoming a crucial offensive against the Hindenburg Line. The Allies successfully breached the German line despite heavy resistance and captured St. Quentin

John Brockman.

Canal. This battle, together with other assaults along the Hindenburg Line, showed the Germans that the end was near. Doughboy Brockman was marginally wounded from fragment of a bursting shell. In April 1919, he was honorably discharged at Camp Owen Burne, Texas, with the notation "Character Excellent."

Russell Vaughan.

RUSSELL VAUGHAN of Lordsburg in Hidalgo County was a mine engineer in civilian life. In November 1917, he enlisted at Fort Bliss and became part of the Quartermaster Corps (QMC) unit. Soldiers depend on the QMC for logistical support in the battlefield. The mission of the QMC is to produce, acquire and sustain the general supply for the army that is so crucial for victory.

Vaughan sailed for France in September 1918 and, like many soldiers, became seasick on the voyage and was happy to see land. Recovered and ready, doughboy Vaughan arrived in Brest, France. From there, he traveled with his unit to Dijon, France. Soon after, he was positioned and performed QMC functions in Neufchateau, Rimaucourt and Le Mans.

In July 1919, he sailed on a steamer to New York, traveling to San Antonio for discharge. Army veteran Vaughan resumed his work as an engineer in New Mexico.

Mont. C. Allison.

MONT. C. ALLISON of Lea County, in southeastern New Mexico at the Texas border, was a farmer before being drafted in August 1918. He went to Camp Cody and was assigned to Company G, 133rd Infantry, 34th Division.

In October 1918, aboard an old English freighter, Allison traveled to Liverpool, England. At Southampton, he crossed the English Channel to Le Havre, France. He was trained, equipped and ready to fight the German army, but the armistice ended that objective.

Doughboy Allison was one of thousands of men who arrived in the fall of 1918 ready for action just when the war ended. He was stationed in the village of Stenay; the U.S. Army captured the town before 1100 hours on November 11.

SECOND LIEUTENANT BENJAMIN I. BERRY of Lincoln County, located in the central region of New Mexico, was with Company A, 5th Machine Gun Battalion. In October 1918, he exhibited extraordinary leadership abilities at Mont Blanc, France.

When his company captain was killed commanding an outpost, Berry rushed to the position to take charge. During this action, he sustained a serious head wound and was ordered to evacuate the field. Instead, he removed the surgeon's evacuation tag and rejoined his company to fight.

Lieutenant Berry resumed his leadership and command of the defense for twenty-four hours. When the company was relieved, he led his men back to the trenches. For this brave action, he received the Distinguished Service Cross and the *Croix de Guerre*. Lieutenant Berry died of his wounds on November 20, 1918.

Robert Hale.

ROBERT HALE was from the town of Carrizozo in Lincoln County. Lawrence Murphy, a leader in the 1878 Lincoln County War, was a ranch owner in Carrizozo. Hale enlisted in the army with the 25th Engineers in January 1918. After a few months in army camps, he departed the United States at Hoboken, New Jersey, and sailed for France.

At St. Nazaire, the engineers went to work building roads and warehouses. When the job was done, they left for the front lines. The next job was repairing roads and bridges on which ambulances carried wounded men to aid stations. Then the men marched to Malancourt to camp and set up a staging area for building ammunition dumps in Montfaucon. The engineers built narrow-gauge railways leading to the Argonne Forest.

Doughboy Hale had a close call from German aero planes, as described in his own words:

> We were coming from work going to our camp just merrily marching along the road when the Jerry aero planes took after us. Looking for a place to hide, a nearby log was the only thing I could use for protection. The only thing I did was stick my head under the log. The machine gun bullets were hitting all around me but none of them had my number.

The engineers continued their construction and repair work until the end of the war and beyond. In May 1919, Hale sailed from France on the SS *Kaiserin Auguste Victoria*. On the morning of May 25, Hale and the other returning doughboys saw the Statue of Liberty: "Can never explain how good the sight of the U.S.A. was to me."

First Lieutenant Paul Frank Baer was from Columbus in Luna County, in southwestern New Mexico, near the Mexican border. As part of a new unit in the AEF, he was assigned to the 103rd Aero Squadron. All previous wars were waged on land and/or oceans. In World War I, "flying machines" demanded the attention of the military.

At the start of the war, planes were used for aerial photography and reconnaissance. Over time, the military identified additional benefits, and so did Lieutenant Baer and his fighter plane. His aggressiveness in the skies brought down at least eight German planes. For his action in the skies over Reims, France, Lieutenant Baer was awarded a Bronze Oak Leaf for extreme bravery in the air.

Everett E. Cowgill from Columbus in Luna County was with Company C, 16th Infantry Regiment, and was stationed at the Presidio in San Francisco. In April 1914, the 16th was transferred to Fort Bliss in reaction to the border conflicts. Two years later, the regiment went to Columbus after the Villa raid. Cowgill entered Old Mexico with Pershing, the 6th Infantry and 13th Cavalry as part of the Mexican Punitive Expedition. In February 1917, the expedition returned to the United States at Columbus and moved via motor trucks to Fort Bliss.

A few months later, doughboy Cowgill and his unit sailed to France, arriving at the port of St. Nazaire, a central receiving place for supplies and soldiers. The men trained for a period of time before moving into action. In March 1918, he went into the trenches to stop a big German drive.

Everett E. Cowgill.

In May, Cowgill was at the front engaged in the first U.S. offensive at the Battle of Cantigny. In July, the Americans assisted the French at Soissons; U.S. soldiers drove through the German right flank, cutting communications and causing a retreat from the Marne Salient that was aimed at Paris. The Allies recaptured ground lost in the German Spring Offensive.

Cowgill moved on to the St. Mihiel Offensive and was wounded by a high-explosive shell. He spent the rest of the war and beyond the armistice in a French hospital. In August 1919, doughboy Cowgill returned to America and New Mexico.

THOMAS G. LACKLAND was a prospector and miner in Luna County before entering the army and reporting to officers training camp in Leon Springs, Texas. He was commissioned a captain of field artillery in November 1917. In the previous year, Lackland was engaged in Columbus, New Mexico, subsequent to the Villa raid. He entered Old Mexico with a column of men as a guide and scout.

Captain Lockland arrived in Europe in July 1918. His unit, the 90th Division, relieved the 1st Division at the St. Mihiel Salient at 0800 hours on August 24, prepared for action and engaged the Germans, accomplishing all objectives ahead of schedule. Then Captain Lockland and the division moved to the Lucey Sector, ready for the Meuse-Argonne Offensive; the 90th Division entered the line on October 21.

In the final two weeks of the war, the 90th was engaged at Sivry, La Perche, Cierges, Briesulles-sur-Meuse and, on Armistice Day, Sassey-sur-Meuse. The following excerpt is from Major General Henry T. Allen, division commander:

The division commander had no adequate words to express his great satisfaction and delight with the fine military spirit of the division, and his pride in its fighting value after seventy-four days (less an interval of seven days) in the fighting lines....In spite of the severe losses and terrific demands that these successes have extracted, the indomitable spirit and keenness to fight continue to characterize the division. Every member of this gallant force has a right to be proud of the services he has rendered in a great cause of human liberty. Our country may count with assurance upon the execution with success of whatever duty it may entrust of the 90th Division.

Each soldier's story is based on personal accounts from their time in the army. Each photograph provides quiet testament to the drama and impressions of their experiences. As veterans, their responses to the New Mexico state archivist's survey are a valuable part of history that shows their efforts in winning the war.

Chapter 9

The Home Front

In times of war, soldiers on the front lines depend on their nation's citizens to provide support needed for victory. War is not exclusively military business; civilians are essential in producing war materiel demanded at the front—the job of the home front.

During the First World War, the United States needed to change its peacetime perspective—military and civilian. When Congress voted to declare war on Germany, the U.S. Army had fewer than 200,000 men. This state of readiness led to the Wilson administration's introduction of the Selective Service Act. Secretary of War Newton Baker selected the first draft number. Americans from across the country answered the call; the act produced millions of draftees and volunteers. Among with the men were more than 16,000 New Mexicans. Eventually, the United States mobilized 4 million soldiers, with 2 million deployed to France.

Army training camps were established, including Camp Cody, located near Deming, New Mexico, and the Atchison, Topeka & Santa Fe and the Southern Pacific railway lines. It was called Camp Deming before it was renamed for Buffalo Bill Cody, who died in 1917. During the war, thirty thousand men were trained at Camp Cody.

Combat training seemed to be geared to the methods of the Spanish-American War in Cuba and not to the modern warfare in France. That training lag would end. Adjustments were needed to address the weapons and methods that would be found in France. Camp Cody provided training for National Guard units from the Midwest states: North and

South Dakota, Iowa, Minnesota and Nebraska. These units became the 34th Infantry Division and were called the Sandstorm Division, given the desert environment.

The U.S. Navy had work to do as well. Navy ships were focused on Mexico, and the two best battleships, the *Texas* and the *New Mexico*, were not battle-tested. U.S. warships were undermanned, and the navy had few anti-submarine ships. That situation started a long-term building program for the navy.

In April 1917, with Congressional authority, President Wilson established federal agencies employing thousands of workers to bring the country to a war footing in terms of production and morale. Of particular interest was the Committee on Public Information (CPI). The purpose of the CPI was to manage war information. Some called it prowar propaganda; others called it patriotism designed to help the war effort. In any case, anti-German pamphlets demonized the German kaiser and his army.

Not all Americans were behind the preparedness movement. Progressives saw war as driven by big business. Banker J.P. Morgan loaned millions to Great Britain. War materiel makers such as Bethlehem Steel and DuPont would make millions of dollars from warfare. Americans citizens who were encouraged to buy Liberty Bonds also financed the war.

The motion picture industry produced propaganda films including *The Kaiser, the Beast of Berlin*. U.S. propaganda portrayed the Germans as evil Huns. Hamburgers became "liberty sandwiches." World War I started modern propaganda that expanded during World War II, with greater reach, frequency and impact. In addition, German culture in the United States was under pressure, with churches and schools eliminating the use of the language. German citizens had to register with the government and carry identification cards. The more than two thousand people who were accused of spying or helping Germany were imprisoned; all were released after the war.

In June, the U.S. Congress passed the Espionage Act of 1917, designed to prevent any support of Germany. The law prohibited interfering in military matters and aiding the enemies of America. The following May, the Espionage Act was extended with the Sedition Act to cover negative speech about the war effort or prevent the sale of war bonds. The act was repealed in 1920.

Constitutionality and interpretation of the law were immediate issues of concern. It was clearly a controversial law. Many argued that it was, at the least, an offense to the U.S. Constitution. Others argued that it was needed to protect the American people during the Great War. The American Protective League worked to identify suspected German sympathizers and antiwar activists. It was a private organization connected to the Federal Bureau of Investigation.

On July 30, 1916, there was an explosion on a New Jersey pier. The Black Tom munitions depot detonation was thought to be sabotage by German agents and part of Germany's secret war against America. Also, the March 1917 explosion at the Mare Island Naval Shipyard in California was believed to be the work of German saboteurs.

America was not exactly neutral before declaring war on Germany. Based on prewar relationships with England and France, the United States was inclined to support the Allies. Also, Germany's policies of aggression and expansion were in conflict with American values, real or perceived. The German blockade was very real. The glaring U.S. exports to England and France (and *not* Germany) partially motivated Berlin. German agents and saboteurs conducted covert operations in the United States to stop shipments of war supplies to their enemies.

There was a name linked to the acts of sabotage in New Jersey and in California: Lothar Witzke. In February 1918, Witzke was arrested while crossing the border from Mexico in Nogales, Arizona. He was carrying a coded letter identifying him to the imperial consular of the Republic of Mexico. He was convicted and sentenced to death by a court-martial but instead was deported to Germany in 1923.

U.S. Food Administration leader Herbert Hoover encouraged all Americans to economize on food and grow victory gardens. Efficient management of the country's food distribution was an important wartime goal. Although "Rosie the Riveter" achieved iconic stature during World War II, many American women worked in traditional men's jobs in World War I as well. For the first time in U.S. history, women filled the ranks in factories to produce war supplies. They manned streetcars, worked on farms and, in some areas, were employed as police officers. Also, women joined the Red Cross to help soldiers and their families. The entire country, not just the military, was at war.

By March 1918, the War Industries Board, led by financier Bernard Baruch, operated using a business rather than governmental approach to production. The U.S. government mobilized human and economic resources for the war industries. Wartime America would operate in full gear.

Although it was not the first time the national anthem was played at a baseball game, it gained prominence in the 1918 World Series, with Boston facing off against the Chicago Cubs. In the seventh-inning stretch, the band played "The Star-Spangled Banner." Boston third baseman, Fred Thomas, a doughboy on leave from active duty, saluted. Other players placed their hands to their hearts. This tradition has continued for World Series and holiday games for years and then ultimately for every game.

Governor Ezequiel C. de Baca was succeeded by Washington E. Lindsey in Santa Fe. Governor Lindsey was a "War Executive" who created a committee designed to manage New Mexico's resources. The committee would provide for state and national security during the war. Subsequently, the New Mexico legislature enacted the Public Defense Act, which replaced the war committee. New Mexico's human, agricultural, economic and military resources received increased management and organization to protect America.

From the Public Defense Act came the Council of Defense, a nine-member council appointed by the governor. It was responsible for the production and conservation of food crops and animals and for the growth of the army. Among the many civilian organizations to campaign for war funds were the Knights of Columbus, the YMCA and the Salvation Army. Overall, citizens of the new state of New Mexico offered full support of America's efforts in the Great War.

Europe had a different story on the home front. Discontent was evident in German, French and British societies. There were many hardships for German civilians. The Allied naval blockade led to hunger in the general population. Coal and clothing on the home front were in short supply. National morale was negatively affected by the shortage of the basic elements of life. Some claimed that decreasing home front support led to Germany's defeat in the field. Conversely, others claimed that after the Hindenburg Line was attacked, the home front support collapsed.

In France, a foreign invasion and occupation caused anxiety. With the German army in Flanders, the French were fighting to exist as an independent country. Parisians endured air raids, shelling and an enemy who was dangerously close to Paris in 1914 and 1918. Also, food shortages added to the strain of the population. Extensive employment of women compensated for the desperate shortage of manpower at home.

Similar to France, Britain was war-weary by 1918. German air raids caused apprehension and led to the formation of the Royal Air Force. Moreover, the Atlantic U-boat campaign against Allied shipping created shortages in supplies. Millions of British women also worked in munitions productions.

New Mexican women were aware of the war efforts made by the English and French women and became one of the first communities (if not the first) in the United States to mobilize for war service. In May 1917, the New Mexico Council of Defense created the Women's Auxiliary. New Mexico's first lady was appointed as leader. During a meeting in Santa Fe, they organized and aligned their group with the national goals. The women released a flyer that read, in part, "To bring together in friendly and efficient cooperation all of the women's organizations in the country now doing or desiring to do patriotic work."

Later named the Women's Committee, the group was highly successful and contributed to New Mexico's war record with zeal, confidence and sacrifice. Among the projects initiated by the committee were victory gardens, open markets and drives for Liberty Loans. Tens of thousands of dollars were raised for the war effort. Also, the women showed success in collecting supplies from towns and Indian pueblos.

To encourage the projects, communication channels between New Mexico women and the government were established via letters and newspapers. In this early form of networking, the New Mexico press offered enthusiastic leadership in supporting the Women's Committee and the United States winning the war.

New Mexico National Guard (NMNG)

The New Mexico National Guard artillery batteries were renowned AEF units and served with distinction in France. Originally known as the 1st Territorial Militia or the New Mexico Volunteers, the unit became the NMNG in 1897. The NMNG, which served in Cuba during the war with Spain, was active as part of the Mexican Punitive Expedition and on the Mexican border.

The Columbus, New Mexico raid led to the National Defense Act of 1916 that federalized and mobilized National Guard units from the states, including New Mexico. During the U.S.-Mexican border war, the 1st New Mexico Field Artillery arrived in Columbus as the first National Guard unit to respond.

In April 1917, after the border war and guarding the border, America and the new state of New Mexico faced a historic event: the United States declared war on Germany. Nine hundred NMNG soldiers mustered out of federal service just before declaration. Of that number, many served in World War I with the valuable experience obtained in the Mexican conflict.

The 1st Regiment of Infantry of the NMNG was mobilized for World War I by the federal government and was sent to Camp Kearny in California. The New Mexico men were merged with Arizona and California National Guard men within the 40th U.S. Army Division. From Camp Kearny, the California division was sent to La Guerche, France. When the division arrived in France, the men actively trained replacement soldiers for the Western Front—a vital job given the attrition rate of the war. Other assignments were POW guard duty, maintaining ambulance service and performing depot responsibilities. Also, the 21st Regiment of Railway Engineers included many New Mexicans who had worked for the Santa Fe Railway.

In addition to doughboys serving in the NMNG, thousands of other New Mexicans joined the regular army or were drafted. General James Baca, National Guard commander, directed the draft and enlisted activities on a statewide basis. As a result, New Mexico ranked fifth in providing men per capita. Overall, National Guard units were a significant part of the AEF.

Chapter 10

New Mexico Doughboys II

S oldier stories in this section address McKinley, Mora, Otero, Quay, Rio Arriba, Roosevelt, Sandoval and San Juan Counties. The corresponding county seats are Gallup, Mora, Alamogordo, Tucumcari, Tierra Amarilla, Portales, Bernalillo and Aztec.

★★★

In 1914, the U.S. Army relied on horses and wagons for military transport of artillery, ammunition and supplies. General Pershing's motorized expedition into Mexico (see chapter 3) showed the value of motor power that carried over to Europe. The first arrival of doughboys in France included truck companies of seventy men and thirty trucks. U.S. armies were rolling with armored cars and trucks, ambulances and ammunition/supply transport trucks. Ultimately, the AEF operated thousands of motor vehicles, driven by determined doughboys.

LOUIS BOSTOT of McKinley County, located on New Mexico's border with Arizona, was one of those doughboys. Bostot, inducted in the army in May 1918, was assigned to the 2nd Field Artillery Supply Company.

When he arrived in France, he drove army supply trucks day and night. The trucks driven by soldiers required hazardous hand-cranked starts and strong legs to engage the mechanical brakes. There were no rear-view mirrors

Louis Bostot.

or windshields. After the war, the army experience contributed to the extensive growth of motor vehicles and of truck transport in the United States. After the general disbandment of the army, he went home to New Mexico and worked as a chauffeur.

Doughboy HERCULANO BACA was a rancher in Mora County, located in northeastern New Mexico, when he enlisted in August 1917. Baca, of Shoemaker, New Mexico, became part of the Battery A, Field Artillery.

In May 1918, he was on a transport from Hoboken, New Jersey, to La Nazaire, France. After months of training in France, Baca and his unit started for the front and went into action at Château-Thierry near La Perle Farm. At midnight on July 14, the guns of Baca's battery opened up—it was the Second Battle of the Marne. The battery pounded the German lines at Aisne-Marne and the Ourcy-Vesle River.

In September, the battery returned to the front at St. Mihiel and blasted back in action. Baca and Battery A, Field Artillery, participated in the last chapter of the war, the Meuse-Argonne Campaign. They were engaged near Montzeville and stayed until November 11, 1918. After the armistice, doughboy Baca's unit attached to the 3rd Army and followed the retreating Germans through France, Belgium and Luxembourg. Finally, the 3rd Army arrived in Germany as an occupying force.

After the war, the Meuse-Argonne American Cemetery and Memorial, the largest American cemetery in Europe, was founded near the village of Romange. The cemetery contains more than fourteen thousand American military graves. Most of the fallen were killed at the Meuse-

Herculano Baca *(far right)*, with doughboys.

Argonne Offensive, including DAVID YAZZA, a Navajo Indian from McKinley County.

Doughboy Yazza was killed in action while on reconnaissance for army regiments of the 5th Division about to cross the Meuse River. General Pershing called the crossing of the Meuse, while under fire, one of the most brilliant feats in the history of the American army in France. Then the regiments participated in ending the war.

While collecting information preceding the crossing, doughboy Yazza was killed by German machine gun fire, as described in the official report:

> *Yazza was a scout in my patrol on Hill 201 at Clery Le Grand on November 2, 1918 at 3 P.M. five machine guns opened on us when we were on our way back after reaching enemy lines and obtaining the information we were sent after. We were within 30 ft. of 2 of the machine guns when they opened fire and Yazza dropped killed instantly.*
>
> *Informant Blackwell, WM. Sgt.*
> *Co. M 60th Inft Peralto, NM*
> *Sgd. H.R. Tune Captain 60th Inf.*

Also, the following notice appeared in the *Gallup Independent*:

> *David Yazza a Navajo Indian whose home was at Crownpoint was recently killed in action in France while fighting the Hun for freedom for all nations. Agent S.F. Stacher at Crownpoint received notification of his supreme sacrifice from Washington D.C.*

BENJAMIN GONZALES of Mora Country was a wagoner in Company D, 3rd Ammunitions Train. Horse-drawn wagons required a skilled wagoner to manage transportation on bad roads filled with a jumble of trucks and wagons. The wagoners often operated in bad weather and under enemy fire.

In July 1918, near Château-Thierry, he witnessed three soldiers killed, with others wounded, while removing company records that were about to be captured by the Germans. Gonzales jumped in a truck and raced to load the records and wounded men and then drove back the U.S. lines under heavy shell fire. Doughboy Gonzales was awarded the Distinguished Service Cross for bravery in this action.

FILIBERTO VIALPANDO was from Wagon Mound in Mora County. The town is near Wagon Mound Butte, a landmark for covered wagons traveling along the Santa Fe Trail.

In April 1918, Vialpando went overseas to England, France and finally to Germany. While on the Western Front, he was part of the 355th Infantry Regiment, 89th Division; the division was part of the Battle of St. Mihiel in September 1918. The advancing doughboys forced a German retreat and continued in action in Meuse-Argonne Offensive. Doughboy Vialpando was on the front lines six times. After being discharged at Fort Bliss, he returned to New Mexico.

ROSALIO BALDONADO of Alamogordo in Otero County, located in southern New Mexico at the Texas state line, was a high school graduate at the time of his enlistment in June 1918. He attended the U.S. Auto Mechanics School, a branch of the University of Texas–Austin. Then he arrived at Camp John Wise in San Antonio, a training facility for U.S. Army balloon crews. He was assigned to the 54th Balloon Company. Observation balloons were used for aerial intelligence and artillery identification on the Western Front. The manned balloons conducted more than 1,500 combat ascensions.

From Texas, Baldonado was sent with the 54th Balloon Company to Newport News, Virginia. Camp Morrison was an embarkation point for

Rosalio Baldonado.

Edward Behringer.

soldiers on the way to France. Along with his unit, he received overseas equipment. They were ready to leave for France when the armistice was signed. Doughboy Baldonado was discharged as a sergeant in December before going home to New Mexico.

EDWARD BEHRINGER, from Piñon in Otero County, worked in ranching (stock) before his induction. He completed Officer's Training School in Camp Funston. Upon arrival in France, he attended "Gas School" in Chatillon-sur-Seine.

In August/September 1918, he was assigned to the 89th Division in the Toul Sector and was up front in the battles of St. Mihiel and of Meuse-Argonne. In October, Behringer was transferred to the 1st Army and stationed in Commercy, France.

While on detached service with the British, he attended military police school and became an MP instructor in the 2nd Army, remaining there until the armistice. Then his unit was ordered to 3rd Army Headquarters in Germany.

From there, doughboy Behringer joined an MP Battalion in Luxembourg. In July 1919, he was promoted to first sergeant of Company B of the battalion. After discharge at Camp Dix in New Jersey, he went home to New Mexico and resumed his ranching work.

Doughboy HUGH K. GALE of Quay County, which borders Texas, was with the 8th Machine Gun Battalion in France. On October 4, 1918, he was killed in action. Gale was posthumously awarded the Distinguished Service Cross as detailed in War Department General Orders No. 16 (1920):

The President of the United States of America, authorized by Act of Congress, July 9, 1918, takes pride in presenting the Distinguished Service Cross (Posthumously) to Private Hugh K. Gale (A.S.N: 1622152), United States Army, for extraordinary heroism in action while serving with Company C, 8th Machine-Gun Battalion, 3d Division, A.E.F., north of Cierges, France, 4 October 1918. When the attack on Hill 241 was held up, Private Gale led a few infantrymen and machine gunners forward under artillery and machine-gun fire to establish a new line about a kilometer in advance of our front lines. He was mortally wounded while making the dash forward.

Adolf Abeyta.

ADOLF ABEYTA of Quay County was assigned to the 21st Engineers. The Army Engineer Corps was in great demand. In fact, there were more than 350,000 engineers in France, providing priceless support for the Allied armies. Army engineers built bridges across rivers and were responsible for building roads, digging trenches, repairing train tracks and placing barbed wire in the field. Also, engineers constructed many types of support buildings and shelters.

In September 1918, doughboy Abeyta and his company assembled to prepare for the St. Mihiel operation. On the morning of offensive, September 12, they moved out. There was a great deal to be done. The company handled and moved large numbers of men and equipment, vital to the success of the offensive.

On October 30, the company approached the town of Romagne, still held by the Germans, and endured a shell attack close to its position. The next morning, a barrage started directly in front of the men. At 0400 hours, the company rolled light packs, had a cold breakfast and started to the town by following the line of advance. Abeyta recalled that morning:

As we were entering this town the lines of advance were just going over the hill at a little town called Bouthieville about two kilometers ahead. The buildings in Romagne seemed to be hopping around like corn in a hopper,

Adolf Abeyta (*far left*), with doughboys.

the walls falling on all sides of us and clouds of dust arising everywhere. Many ambulances were rushing to the rear filled with killed or wounded. Many prisoners passed us on the road carrying their dead and wounded. The artillery fire was intense. The third platoon proceeded along the line to the right of Romange towards St. Georges. Dead men and horses covered the ground on all sides. A detachment of the 16th Engineers were brought up to give us assistance. They had no sooner relieved us at that place when a large shell exploded among them killing four privates and the lieutenant in command. The first and second platoons continued to move forward on the road leading to Montigney and Dun sur Meuse. The artillery fire was the heaviest we had experienced. Every man escaped death by a hair's breadth a hundred times this day but providence still protected us.

Following the Allied victory, the division worked on standard-gauge railways. In February 1919, doughboy Abeyta and his unit were relieved, ending their railroad work in France. In May, the USS *President Grant* carried the engineers back to the United States.

GREGORIO SANCHEZ, from the town of Dixon in Rio Arriba County, entered the service in October 1917. Rio Arriba is in northern New Mexico at the Colorado state line. He was sent to Camp Funston and Camp Kearny for infantry training.

In June 1918, Sanchez sailed from Hoboken, New Jersey, to Liverpool, England. Upon arrival in France, he joined Company M, 30th Infantry, 3rd U.S. Army. The next month, Sanchez was engaged at the Battle of Aisne-Marne and at the Veisle Sector. He continued to fight at the St. Mihiel Offensive and in the Argonne, the final battles of the war. The 3rd Army remained in Europe with the Army of Occupation until September 1919.

Doughboy Sanchez and his unit returned to the United States. He was discharged at Fort Bliss and went home to New Mexico.

Gregorio Sanchez.

Patricio Chavez.

PATRICIO CHAVEZ was from the community of Chimayo, located north of Santa Fe in Rio Arriba and Santa Fe Counties and near the Sangre de Cristo Mountains. He enlisted in the army in October 1917 and was sent to Camp Funston. In June 1918, he was in France with Company H, 110th Infantry Regiment, 28th Division.

Chavez went into action and fought at the Battle of Château-Thierry for five days. Aero planes dropped sacks of bread into the trenches to relieve the hunger of the men. Company H went "over the top," and within four hours, 250 men were killed or wounded. Chavez was shot twice through the hip. When four men were dragging him away on a blanket, they were killed, leaving him on the battlefield. Four other men were successful in taking him to a hospital. With care from the Red Cross nurses and a few months, Chavez recovered and returned to the front. This time, he was shot in the hand. Doughboy Chavez was decorated for bravery at the Battle of Château-Thierry.

ROBERT WHITE of Portales in Roosevelt County, located in the eastern part of New Mexico at the Texas state line, was a locomotive engineer before enlisting in the army in August 1917. Doughboy White lost his left arm in the war against the kaiser.

On May 12, 1918, he wrote to his mother from Hospital 9 AEF. It was Mother's Day, a new holiday. The second Sunday in May became Mother's Day in 1914. His letter was published in a Portales newspaper under the heading "Wounded in France," reading in part:

> At last the war has come home to the people of this community. R.E. White…has written a brave letter to his mother….Mr. White, when he arrives, will find that the people of this community appreciate what he has done in the war; they will prove to him that they are grateful that he held up the honor of the community. The letter appears below:

Dear Mother,

I wrote a day or two ago, but will not miss Mother's Day....I suppose you have my letter by this time telling you of the loss of my left arm. I am up and running around and getting along fine....Everybody over here seems to feel confident that the allies have the high hand on the Bache. We will hope so. I wish I could have done more....I feel much better on having been here and having done my bit, even though I lost my arm, than if I stayed at home....As I am through over here I will be so happy when I can be back among my loved ones. I hope this will find you well as it did last year and I that will have the opportunity of writing you for many years to come.

Your loving son, Prva. R.E. White

Robert White.

It happened near Côte de Mormont, France, in the last week of the war. WILLIAM H. SWEARINGEN of Roosevelt County was with the Medical Detachment, 315th Infantry, in France when he heard a call for help from no man's land. He answered the call and responded with heroism by ignoring the incessant machine gun fire and snipers. Reaching the man, he gave first aid and found cover. After dark, he carried the wounded man back to the American lines. For this action, doughboy Swearingen was awarded the Distinguished Service Cross.

On September 4, 1918, OREN O. CROCKETT started a night hike to the St. Mihiel Sector, arriving on the morning of September 12. Doughboy Crockett of Plainview in Roosevelt County entered the sector in time for a great barrage. The Americans fought back the "Dutch" for fifteen to twenty miles in the following days. Then, after the Argonne success, the U.S. soldiers followed the "Dutchmen" into Germany. Crockett played a vital role as a trench runner or messenger. Runners, who wore a red armband, provided messages from one command to another with speed and precision. They were required to know front-line areas, read maps and reconnoiter. In

Oren O. Crockett (*right*).

February 1920, Crockett received the following letter from the Adjutant General's Office in Washington, dated February 25, 1920:

Mr. Oren O. Crockett
Plainview, New Mexico

Dear Sir:—
The War Department has awarded you the Distinguished Service Cross for extraordinary heroism in action as per the accompanying citation.
*   The Quartermaster General of the Army has been directed to forward the cross for you to the Recruiting Officer, Albuquerque, N.M., who will cause the same to be presented to you.*

Very Truly Yours,
P.C. Harris, The Adjutant General

CITATION

Oren O. Crockett, runner, Company C. 8th Machine Gun Battalion, for extraordinary heroism in action north of Cierges, France, October 4, 1918. Private Crockett, during an attack under terrific shell and machine gun fire, carried messages from company to platoon headquarters, thus maintaining the necessary communication required in a successful operation.

Crockett was honorably discharged in El Paso, Texas. He returned home to New Mexico and resumed his occupation as farmer and rancher. He appears in the photo here with a sailor.

CORPORAL ALBERT D. MALLET was from the town of Bernalillo in Sandoval County. The county is located in northeastern New Mexico adjacent to Santa Fe and Bernalillo Counties. Mallet entered the army in January 1918. Mallet was a second-generation French immigrant. When he arrived in France, it was a homecoming insofar as his father, Pierre Mallet, was French-born. He would find a great irony as an American infantryman.

Doughboy Mallet fought on the same battleground as his father did in the Franco-Prussian War of 1870–71. France lost that war to Germany, which was under Prussian control. He hoped that history would not repeat itself—it did not.

Guadalupe Fragua.

Battista Targhetta.

GUADALUPE FRAGUA, an American Indian, was from Jemez Pueblo in Sandoval County, located fifty miles northwest of Albuquerque. Jemez Pueblo, the last Towa-speaking pueblo, is surrounded by red sandstone mesas and is part of the Jemez Mountain trail.

Doughboy Fragua was eighteen years old and attended the Santa Fe Indian School before entering the army. He served as a bugler and combat engineer in France.

BATTISTA TARGHETTA from Sandoval County joined the U.S. Army in 1917 as an infantryman and was sent to Camp Funston. Some months later, doughboy Targhetta sailed to England and across the channel to France. He joined Company D, 9th Infantry, 2nd "Indian Head" Division, and was engaged at St. Mihiel and the Meuse-Argonne Offensives in the drive to end the war.

In October 1918, the division was closely engaged at the Battle of Mont Blanc Ridge near Reims, France. The Indian Head Division faced several German divisions and captured the ridge; the Germany army was thrown out of the Champagne region.

CORPORAL AUGUSTIN MARTINEZ, from San Juan County, received the Distinguished Service Cross. In addition, he received the *Croix de Guerre*.

On August 4, 1918, Doughboy Martinez of Company I, 356th Infantry, arrived in Brocq, France, and was assigned to regimental reserves. Two weeks later, he went into the first-line trenches. After a brief rotation period, he returned to the front lines on September 9 at St. Mihiel, Lucey Sector.

At 1700 hours on September 11, 1918, Martinez and his regiment were notified that at 0500 hours they were going over the top. The men were equipped with 220 rounds of ammunition, hand and rifle grenades and wire cutters. At 0100 hours on September 12, the American barrage started and continued until 0455 hours—five minutes before entering no man's land. The Americans opened up with five minutes of machine gunning. Then, at 0500 hours sharp, the captain yelled, "Over the top, boys."

In his own words, Martinez described what happened next: "[A]nd over the top we went with the most pleasure and dignity ever seen. We went on continuous advancing for two days and nights...then we took our positions on the right of the St. Mihiel front."

On October 19, doughboy Martinez and his regiment advanced to the Meuse-Argonne. Along with four other

Augustin Martinez.

men, Martinez made a flank attack on a heavy machine gun emplacement. In the face of fire, they charged the position, overpowered the enemy and captured the guns. Martinez pursued the retreating Germans until they were lost in the fog of war.

On November 1, the Americans broke the German lines and advanced until November 11. After the German surrender, his division became part of the occupying force in Europe. His army experience is reflected in his own words to the New Mexico state archivist: "I am pretty well satisfied of my experiences...so I remain your best citizen of New Mexico and of the Spanish-American soldiers of the state."

JOSE BENJAMIN ARCHULETA, from San Juan County, was a friend of Augustin Martinez. Archuleta was with the 356th Infantry Regiment, organized in August 1917 and assigned to the 89th Division at Camp Funston. He traveled with the division to Camp Mills in New York.

On June 3, 1918, from Hoboken, New Jersey, the 356th boarded the British ship *Coronial*. The steamer left the pier and sailed down the Hudson River and neared the Statue of Liberty. On the Atlantic, the *Coronial* had protection from U-boat attacks by U.S. Navy warships.

Approaching Europe, the ship sailed near Ireland and down the Irish Sea to Liverpool, England. Then they crossed the channel to Le Havre, France. The 89th Division became part of the Lorraine, St. Mihiel and Meuse-Argonne operations. Doughboy Archuleta was wounded on the battlefield.

F.W. Townsend.

FREDERICK W. TOWNSEND, from Aztec in San Juan County, was part of the 656th Air Squadron. In January 1918, Lieutenant Townsend arrived at Camp Garden City in Long Island, New York, where he and his unit were fully equipped and moved to the SS *Carpathian*. After landing in Glasgow, Scotland, he traveled on the Great London Northwestern Railroad to Winchester, England. Finally, he sailed from Southampton to Le Havre, France. He was assigned to Clichy, France, outside Paris.

Lieutenant Townsend was given charge of Supply Depot No. 1 Air Service. The following, from an officer's record book, praises his leadership ability:

The undersigned has known Captain Townsend for more than nine months, being his immediate commanding officer. This officer is an excellent administrator and executive, one of the most efficient organization commanders I have known. He is a hard conscientious worker, loyal in the extreme and a most capable leader of men. It is a great pleasure to have had Captain Townsend under my command, as well as a benefit to the service. E. V. Lt. Colonel Sumner, USA.

Soldier stories in this section address San Miguel, Santa Fe, Sierra, Socorro, Taos, Torrance, Union and Valencia Counties. The corresponding county seats are Las Vegas, Santa Fe, Truth or Consequences, Socorro, Taos, Estancia, Clayton and Los Lunas.

★★★

Before the war, JOSÉ GONZALES was a cowboy in San Miguel County, in northeastern New Mexico. In September 1917, he enlisted in the army and was trained at Camp Funston.

In August 1918, Gonzales was at Camp Mills, ready for France. He sailed from New York to Liverpool, England, and to Brest, France. Soon after, he was in the trenches with the 305th Infantry, 77th Division, in Flanders. The next month, units of the 77th Division occupied positions in the trenches at the Argonne. For two months, Gonzales was engaged in the Meuse-Argonne Campaign and was fighting on the front line when the armistice was signed. Doughboy Gonzales was discharged in May 1919, returned to the United States and worked raising stock in New Mexico.

José Gonzales.

SECOND LIEUTENANT LEONARD HOSKINS, 54th Artillery, Coast Artillery Corps, was from East Las Vegas in San Miguel County. On June 29, 1918, Lieutenant Hoskins, positioned at La Chappelle, France, advanced into a shell-swept zone. He searched for wounded soldiers and brought back several men to the American lines. During this time, Doughboy Hoskins was killed. For bravery in action, he was awarded the Distinguished Service Cross.

Lew Springer.

In September 1918, FIRST LIEUTENANT LEW SPRINGER of Las Vegas, in San Miguel County, sailed to France with the 11th Aero Squadron. Due to the lack of planes, he was idle for several months. Then, in July 1918, he was assigned to a Day Bombing Squadron. The aero planes provided reconnaissance information and supported infantry operations. Behind the lines, the squadron conducted bombing attacks on enemy transportation infrastructure, destroying roads, bridges and railways. German war materiel and soldiers also were targets.

The 11th Aero Squadron was awarded battle honors for action at Lorraine, St. Mihiel and the Argonne; Lieutenant Springer was active in those September and October offensives. He was wounded and hospitalized for thirty days in France before arriving in New York in March 1919.

FILADELFIO ARAGON from Sapello, New Mexico, was a farmer before entering the army. The town of Sapello, ten miles north of Las Vegas in San Miguel County, was a trading stop on the Santa Fe Trail.

He enlisted in the army to "lend his services to our government" in August 1918 and arrived at France on November 11, 1918. He was assigned to Company L, 158th Infantry Regiment, 40th Division. The 158th Regiment provided replacements to other regiments and was the honor guard during President Wilson's visit to France.

Doughboy Aragon, who was honorably discharged in May 1919, reflected on his experience in his own words: "El día 29 de octubre de 1918 A.D. abordamos un barco a Brest, Francia. A partir de ahí me trasladaron a la 40ª división del regimiento de infantería 158. Me quedé en Francia por 6 meses. Nos embarcaron en Bordeaux y regresé a América con el mismo regimiento en 17 de abril de 1919 A.D. con honor y gran victoria."

Howell G. Ervien.

HOWELL G. ERVIEN of Santa Fe in Santa Fe County enlisted in Company F, 1st New Mexico Infantry, in June 1917. When commissioned a second lieutenant, he was assigned to Company A at Albuquerque. Lieutenant Ervien moved to Camp Kearny and to the 143rd Machine Gun Battalion, where he was promoted to first lieutenant.

In July 1918, Ervien entrained for Camp Mills; by August, he was in Le Havre, France. Reassigned to the 121st Machine Gun Battalion, 32nd Division, he was engaged in the Meuse-Argonne battles until the end of the war. Then he marched to Germany and remained with the Army of Occupation until April 1919. Doughboy Ervien returned to the United States in May. He sailed from Brest, France, to Boston, arriving at Commonwealth Pier.

SERGEANT ROY H. FLAMM of Santa Fe served in the 1916 Mexican border conflict with Company G, 1ˢᵗ New Mexico Infantry. His grandfather Henry Gottieb von Flamm was a Union soldier in the Civil War who came to America with Carl Schurz, a German revolutionary who became a Union general.

In June 1917, Flamm was among the first twenty thousand U.S. soldiers to land in France. He spent the first five months building American docks in Bordeaux. In January 1918, he was commissioned a lieutenant in the Corps of Engineers and sent to the Toul Sector of the front. While attached to the French army, he was in several battle engagements and received the

Roy H. Flamm.

Croix de Guerre. Also, his French Engineer Regiment received a *Fourragerre*. Doughboy Flamm reflected on his war experience:

> *A great benefit to New Mexico from the war will come in the broader vision or outlook on life it will give many of the so-called Spanish American boys who went abroad and mixed with other elements of our armies. The war will tend to unify us and make us into a more unified nation. I hope the war may be the means of banishing from our midst such terms as Irish-American, German-American, Spanish-America, etc., and that we will all endeavor to emphasize the fact that we are Americans, first, last and all the time. We have all returned from the war better citizens.... We have a larger outlook on life and a desire to be bigger and better than we were before.*

ARCHER W. BEDELL of Santa Fe earned a degree from Trinity College in Hartford, Connecticut. He enlisted in Company F, 1ˢᵗ New Mexico Infantry, and was promoted to quartermaster sergeant. He became a member of the New Mexico Rifle Team, competing in national matches.

In May 1916, he was commissioned second lieutenant, G.O. 10, Office of the Adjutant General, Santa Fe. That same month, he departed for border duty with the regiment. Lieutenant Bedell was appointed engineer officer in the 1st New Mexico Infantry. He mustered out of the army in Columbus prior to the United States entering the war.

Answering the president's call, he reentered the army in May 1917 with the 144th Machine Gun Battalion of the New Mexico National Guard and was promoted to first lieutenant. The battalion sailed from New York to France in July 1918. Once in France, he was assigned to division headquarters for duty in Jonet-sur-L'Aubois, Champs-sur-Marne and Bordeaux. Doughboy Bedell sailed back to New York in April 1919 with a gold chevron for six months of foreign service.

Archer W. Bedell.

In May 1916, MIGUEL DELGADO of Santa Fe served on the Mexican border in Company A, 1st New Mexico Infantry, during the Pershing expedition. It was good experience for his next military challenge in France. He arrived in Brest in July 1918 and soon after was promoted to sergeant in the 11th Veterinary Hospital.

The Army Veterinary Corps Service created a mobile unit for each army division to provide veterinary service for horses, mules and pigeons. Racing Homing pigeons were effectively used to carry messages. It was dangerous for birds flying near enemy soldiers, who would try to shoot down the carrier pigeons and disrupt communications.

Miguel Delgado.

Doughboy Delgado and his unit brought thousands of horses and mules to the front for transportation. Proper care and management of the animals were vital to the war effort. Also, they brought back wounded and gassed animals to the veterinary hospital. His company was credited with being the best veterinary hospital in the AEF.

PATRICIO SANCHEZ of Los Cerrillos in Santa Fe County was a miner in Madrid, New Mexico, before he was called to service in April 1918. By August, he was in France constructing trenches and stringing barbed wire.

In September, doughboy Sanchez was at the front in the Battle of St. Mihiel, where his unit fought for twelve days. The 356th Infantry Regiment rotated out of the fight and then back again to hold the line. The second time on the front, there was more to handle than the Germans. Sanchez described the situation: "We lost our kitchen and provisions train and for six days could not find them and it nearly caused us to starve to death but as it happened we met with a company of aviators in an old village they provided us with bread, cabbage, meat and some carrots."

The regiment was in the trenches again at the Battle of the Argonne, where, according to Sanchez, the men fought like lions for two days. Then he was gassed. Sanchez spent several weeks in hospital before receiving an honorable discharge.

MARSHALL DE BORD of Santa Fe worked with the AT&SF Railroad in Clovis, New Mexico, and the U.S. Surgeon General Office on Santa Fe. Both of his Tennessee grandfathers served in the Civil War. He joined the New Mexico National Guard in 1914 and quickly rose in the ranks, promoted to sergeant, first sergeant, second lieutenant and first lieutenant.

After the Columbus, New Mexico raid by Pancho Villa (see chapter 3), De Bord answered the president's call and served with the border patrol until April 1917. That same month, he answered another presidential call, this time for the war in Europe.

Along with units of the 40th Division, Lieutenant De Bord sailed to France. While in the channel in sight of France, the ship was attacked by a German submarine. The escort British destroyers dropped depth bombs and destroyed the underwater threat.

Once in France, the newly arrived 40th changed from a combat division to a replacement division to supply fresh soldiers to divisions already on the front and provided almost thirty thousand combat replacements, especially important against major German army offensives.

The divisional headquarters was positioned near Verdun and remained there until January 1919. Lieutenant De Bord was honorably discharged from service in June 1919.

JOSE TAFOYA, from the town of Hillsboro in Sierra County, enlisted in the 1st New Mexico Infantry in Albuquerque and was sent to Camp Kearny. In July 1918, he sailed to France, where he was assigned to the 9th Infantry Regiment, 2nd Division, 1st Army.

Tafoya and his regiment were positioned at a quiet sector called Marschebach. The next assignment for the 2nd Infantry was anything but quiet: the division moved St. Mihiel on September 12, 1918 and, on October 3, to the Champagne front at Blanc Mont Ridge. At the end of the battle, the doughboys forced the German army into retreat.

Jose Tafoya.

With victory in hand, the division marched into Germany as part of the Army of Occupation and stayed there until July 1919. Doughboy Tafoya commented on his army experience on November 8, 1919:

> *The Great War has convinced the world that a nation like ours does not need years to prepare for war. It shows that our people are united when our nation is in distress. Where there is union there is strength. One thing I feel sorry about is that we could not have the opportunity to show our patriotism as a regiment of New Mexico. That was the only reason I enlisted in the First New Mexico Infantry. But I am glad that I fought with the famous Second Division. God bless our nation and state of New Mexico.*

Finally, Tafoya and his division were at the Meuse-Argonne front from November 1 to November 11.

Andres Vallejos.

ANDRES VALLEJOS of Socorro County in western New Mexico was engaged in farming in the town of Polvadera before his induction in June 1917. After time in Camp Funston, Camp Kearney and Camp Merrit, he had the standard overseas examination and sailed to France.

Soon after, his unit, the 104th Infantry, 28th Division, was sent to the trenches. At the Battle of Château-Thierry, Vallejos was on the battlefield for five days. On the fifth day, he was wounded. He was shot in the left leg and taken to Hospital 22 in Bordeaux. When released, he went back to the front to be engaged in the Battles of Verdun for six weeks and was wounded again, this time in the right flank. He was taken to Hospital 19 in Paris.

In December 1918, he sailed for Newport News, Virginia, and then to a hospital in Fort Worth, Texas, where he stayed until discharged on January 25, 1919. Doughboy Vallejos was "bound for home sweet home."

EDUARDO GONZALES of Socorro in Socorro County was with Company B, 355th Infantry Regiment, 89th Division. Once in France and in the Rimaucourt area, the division prepared to engage the enemy at the Battle of St. Mihiel. On August 5, 1918, the 89th formed positions at the Toul Sector until September 12, when the attack began. The division attacked and moved through Bois-de-Mort Mare and to Thiaucourt, pushing back a German division as it advanced. The doughboys captured the strongpoint of Bois-de-Mort Mare.

In October, the division with the 5th Army entered the Meuse-Argonne Offensive taking the Bois-de-Bantheville. Then it was hit with gas attacks. German mustard gas shells attacked areas near the division; the shelling was intense, but the men found shelter. Yet supplies were cut off until the evacuation. On November 1, the advance continued; the Americans surged forward, breaking the German lines and forcing the enemy across the Meuse. The doughboys built bridges under heavy fire and continued to pursue the Germans until November 11, 1918.

Eduardo Gonzales.

ABENICIO ROMERO of Taos County, in northern New Mexico on the Colorado border, was a farmer in Rancho de Taos before the war. In May 1918, he arrived in Brest, France, and moved to Soissons, an ancient town near the Aisne River, to join Company C, 18th Infantry Division.

Romero was among the men who launched an offensive at Soissons and the salient that threatened Paris. After that July battle, the Allies recaptured ground lost to the Germans in the Spring Offensive. The Americans suffered 12,000 casualties, the French 107,000 and the Germans 168,000. A German soldier received an Iron Cross medal for action at Soissons—his name was Adolf Hitler.

Doughboy Romero was engaged at the Battles of St. Mihiel and the Meuse-Argonne, where he was wounded and sent to the hospital. The war was over for him and would soon be over for all.

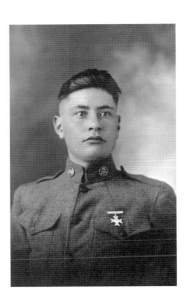
Abenicio Romero.

FLAVIO GONZALES, of Ranchos de Taos in Taos County, was on the front lines at the St. Mihiel Offensive. Doughboy Gonzales wrote about his war experience: "Went to war to fight for our country so that the Germans should not come over here. Had a good treatment in the army—would go back if needed....U.S. is the best country in the world."

ANTONIO BACA of Torrance County was a farmer and stock grower before becoming a soldier. He entered the army in June 1917 and was assigned to the Medical Department/Sanitary Detachment of the 8th Cavalry and achieved the rank of sergeant first class.

Flavio Gonzales.

Baca left the United States with a company of medical men for France. At St. Nazaire, he was assigned to a base hospital; later, he was transferred to the Medical Property Office. In August 1919, doughboy Baca returned to America and related his war experience: "The war...would have brought a permanent peace to the world in general if carried on six months longer. The U.S. entering the war has shown the world the rich resources of our country and with that rapidity the machinery of our country can work when necessary. For New Mexico this war created a better feeling between the Spanish-speaking people and English-speaking people."

FRANCIS BOGGS was from Clayton in Union County, located in the northeastern corner of New Mexico. In July 1919, he sailed to England with a convoy of twelve transport ships and one battleship. Days from Liverpool, six sub-destroyers escorted the convoy to port. During that time, Boggs witnessed a destroyer sink a German submarine. One of the destroyers stayed near the sunken sub until the convoy was off in the distance.

From Southampton, he crossed the channel to Le Havre, France, where he boarded a rail car suited for eight horses or forty men. His letter informed, "The horses would have had more room."

In August, he was assigned to the 8th Machine Gun Battalion; he arrived in Château-Thierry two weeks after the battle and saw the "results or the

Antonio Baca.

remains of the city." In September, his unit was sent to St. Mihiel in support of the advancing Americans as they continued their job at the Argonne Forest on the Verdun Front.

At the front, Boggs and another soldier were given Red Cross armbands and a stretcher to carry wounded men to the first-aid station. The men were busy day and night until Boggs was wounded and his buddy was killed. Boggs said, "I was helping a wounded man when a big six-inch shell landed about six feet from me and put me out of the game. The man I was helping died a few minutes later. Now, don't form the opinion that the Boche would not shoot at a Red Cross man, for they shot at us when we were carrying men on a stretcher."

Doughboy Boggs lost many good friends as he heard "shells bursting around us and machine guns bullets whizz past." For this brave action, he was recommended for the *Croix de Guerre*. He survived his wounds and influenza and returned to New Mexico.

Arriving in Brest, France, in May 1918, LUTHER GARCIA of Union County stayed at the Potassium Barracks of Napoleon Bonaparte. In Blois, France, he was an instructor for Spanish-speaking soldiers from the southern counties of New Mexico. This important job covered battlefield action and the prevention of the effects of German weapons.

Garcia was reassigned to Entreat, France, where he performed intelligence work. In February 1919, he sailed back

Francis Boggs.

Luther Garcia.

to New York. When he disembarked, the Musical League of New York City played the national anthem. The returning doughboys shouted hurrahs to Old Glory.

Paul Borger.

Samuel Hunt.

PAUL BORGER of the town of Amistad, located forty miles south of Clayton in Union County, was a pre-law student before becoming a corporal in the engineering corps. Borger participated in the first phase of the Battle of the Meuse-Argonne at the Meuse River and the capture of Etraya Ridge.

In the battle, he suffered the horrors of a gas attack and was a temporary casualty. Poison gas weapons were especially feared on the Western Front. Whether delivered by an artillery shell or a machine gun, the results were horrendous, leading to instant death or prolonged suffering. One of the most ghastly poisons used was mustard gas. Borger also suffered a second gas attack that required expert medical attention and hospitalization. He was released with impaired vision after a period of total blindness.

In July 1919, Borger sailed to Brooklyn, New York, and was sent to Camp Merritt, New Jersey. Then, in El Paso, doughboy Borger was discharged from the army.

SAMUEL P. HUNT of Des Moines in Union County was a printer and a moving picture operator before entering the service in September 1917. Both of his grandfathers took part in the Civil War, on opposite sides. Both were killed in that war.

Hunt arrived in Liverpool, England, on the English ship *Coronial*. After a series of transports, he was assigned to Versions, France, close to Chaumont; he had two months of training with Company C, 342nd

Machine Gun Battalion, 89th Division, and then moved to the Toul Sector on the front.

He was in the trenches from August to October, engaged at the St. Mihiel Offensive. After the war, the 89th was part of the Army of Occupation. Hunt moved from France to Luxembourg and to Germany. Doughboy Hunt stayed in Germany with his battalion until June 1919. He sailed to New York and went to Camp Upton in Long Island before going back to New Mexico.

Jose de la Cruz Garcia.

JOSE DE LA CRUZ GARCIA was from Valencia County, located in the central region of New Mexico. Days after arriving in France, he was sent to the front lines with his Company H, 30th Infantry Regiment, 3rd Division. It was engaged at the Second Battle of the Marne, or the Aisne-Marne Offensive, in July–August 1918.

The 3rd Division held positions near the Marne River in defense of Paris. The battle resulted from the German Spring Offensive failure. General Ludendorff was hoping for different results from a new strategy.

Although other units retreated, the 3rd Division, including the 30th Regiment, held like a rock—the "Rock of the Marne." The battle was the last German attempt at victory and a turning point that led to the end of the war.

In August, doughboy De la Cruz Garcia was gassed and spent five months in a French hospital before returning to the states. In January 1919, he entered a hospital in Texas with pulmonary tuberculosis; his service ended in March 1919.

Born in Los Lunas, Valencia County, JOSE CASTILLO was part of Company H, 30th Infantry Division. In the final months of the war, he was involved in battles, skirmishes and expeditions in key campaigns leading to the armistice, including the Aisne-Marne Offensive and in the Fismes Sector in the Champagne region. It was a turning point for the Allies.

At midnight on August 6, Castillo and his unit attacked during the Battle of Fismes. The small town of Fismes, now connected by a Memorial Bridge dedicated to the liberating U.S. soldiers, is across the river from the town Fismette. By August 10, that town was captured, but German efforts to retake the town led to two weeks of street battles. The doughboys received heavy machine gun and artillery fire and could not evacuate the wounded. In the end, the Americans held the town.

Doughboy Castillo continued combat action in September at St. Mihiel and, finally, in the Argonne Forest. Although it was the largest military operation in American history, the Meuse-Argonne Offensives have been mostly forgotten in the United States. Those battles that led to the end of the war continued until

Jose Castillo.

11:00 a.m. on November 11, 1918—Armistice Day. The war on the Western Front was over.

The doughboys in this book and all the World War I soldiers are gone. Although they have entered eternity, their stories remain as history and reflect the intrepidness of the Americans in the First World War. The stories of the men on these pages represent the thousands of New Mexico doughboys who crossed the Atlantic and experienced the Great War. Also, soldiers who served in the practically forgotten Siberia expedition were included in this narrative.

Attention was given to every county in New Mexico, with doughboys representing each one. Today, there are almost 200,000 veterans living in New Mexico, about 10 percent of the state's population. The highest percentage of New Mexico veterans are in Catron, Sierra and Otero Counties. Given the large population of Bernalillo, most veterans are in that county.

Monument by Karl Morningstar Illaya, New York.

Whether stated or implied, the stories contained in this project have an element of service, patriotism and pride. The men presented had various military occupational statuses and different war experiences, but all were men of character. Most were citizen-soldiers who served their country and faced a crucial challenge on the world stage. The personal stories were highly effective in making that time vibrant in the mind of this writer—they could do the same for the readers. As the stories reveal, the men lived up to their challenges with extraordinary leadership and courage.

The actions of New Mexico doughboys helped in stopping German aggression and in winning the Great War. The accounts presented are but a small sample that tells a big story—a story worth telling.

November 11, 1918

The Meuse-Argonne Offensive raged on until exactly 11:00 a.m. on November 11. In an ironic parting blow, there were two thousand more casualties before the appointed time. In the French military record, the last entry stated that the war was over—due to victory, not peace. Marshal Foch sent the following message:

> *Official Radio from Paris—6:01 a.m., Nov. 11, 1918.*
> *Marshal Foch to the Commander-in-Chief*
>
> *1. Hostilities will be stopped on the entire front beginning at 11 o'clock, November 11th.*
> *2. The Allied troops will not go beyond the line reached at that hour on that date until further orders.*

In 1919, the armistice was formalized by the Treaty of Versailles. The U.S. Congress officially recognized the end of the war when it passed a concurrent resolution on June 4, 1926, with these words:

> *Whereas the 11th of November 1918, marked the cessation of the most destructive, sanguinary, and far reaching war in human annals and the resumption by the people of the United States of peaceful relations with other nations, which we hope may never again be severed, and*
> *Whereas it is fitting that the recurring anniversary of this date should be commemorated with thanksgiving and prayer and exercises designed*

to perpetuate peace through good will and mutual understanding between nations; and

Whereas the legislatures of twenty-seven of our States have already declared November 11 to be a legal holiday: Therefore be it Resolved by the Senate (the House of Representatives concurring), that the President of the United States is requested to issue a proclamation calling upon the officials to display the flag of the United States on all Government buildings on November 11 and inviting the people of the United States to observe the day in schools and churches, or other suitable places, with appropriate ceremonies of friendly relations with all other peoples.

As a war of attrition, there were no real winners. It did, however, show how national struggles in pursuing national goals can threaten human existence. The world had witnessed unparalleled disaster of massive proportion. Nevertheless, the First World War would not be, as H.G. Wells said, the war to end all wars. One of the bloodiest wars in history was over—temporarily.

The Great War consumed more than 16 million lives. Beyond this shocking statistic, the world experienced aftershocks. Germany's surrender ended the war and started a series of dramatic changes. The scope of conflict provided a source for understanding international events. The empires of Germany, Austria-Hungary, Russia and Turkey were gone. In addition to having an entire generation decimated by war, France endured innumerable loss of assets, as most battles occurred in Flanders. The war's massive expense caused England to be significantly indebted to the United States. This economic factor contributed to the financial center of the world shifting from London to New York. In fact, many national economies, especially Germany's, took a big blow.

For most of the German people, desolation and destitution were the results in the aftermath of the war, with the future uncertain. The most horrifying change would occur fourteen years later. Germany's defeat ended the monarchy and began the Weimar, or Democracy, era. In 1932, the Weimar era was crushed by Nazism.

The First World War was a change agent for America: the United States departed from its policy of non-interventionism in European wars. The U.S. economy was stimulated with increased employment and industrial profits. America emerged as a world power, changing the political and military aspects of global dynamics. In addition, there was widespread discontent with Wilson's wartime policies and with the League of Nations that had an effect on the next presidential election.

In 1920, Democrat Wilson could not run for a third term due to poor health. Theodore Roosevelt, a front runner, died in 1919. Republican senator Warren G. Harding won in a landslide with thirty-seven states, including the first Republican victory in New Mexico.

New technologies were created or enhanced. Motor-powered vehicles would begin to fill the unpaved roads. Aero squadrons pioneered the skies and set the course for civilian air travel. Many women who joined the workforce stayed there after the war. The demands for women to vote gained accelerated traction. In June 1919, Congress passed the Nineteenth Amendment, which gave women the right to vote.

The Great War was over, but not completely for soldiers. The experience probably endured for a lifetime—if you had a life. Many of the men who survived the dreadfulness of the war returned with physical injuries and/or with shell shock from experiencing the advanced killing machines.

Then there was the unfortunate irony of the Bonus Expeditionary Force. In the midst of the Great Depression, more than forty thousand people marched on Washington, D.C., including seventeen thousand World War I veterans. In the summer of 1932, they demanded payment of the promised service certificates. Although the certificates, awarded by the World War Adjusted Compensation Act, were not redeemable until 1945, the so-called Bonus Army wanted/needed payment. Instead, the federal government ordered Washington police to force the veterans to leave their campsite on the lawn of the U.S. Capitol and surrounding areas. Two veterans were shot and killed. President Hoover ordered General MacArthur to end the protest— infantry, cavalry and George Patton's tanks came together on Pennsylvania Avenue. The American army descended on the former doughboys with a cavalry attack, bayonets and tear gas. Veterans and their families were burned out and driven away, unlike any battle they knew in France. In the fall, Hoover lost the White House in a landslide to Franklin D. Roosevelt.

One hundred years later, the Western Front has recovered. Forests that were blown into splinters are forests again; towns that were reduced to rubble are towns once more. Yet the stark realities of war remain as dark and potent reminders. Under the Treaty of Versailles, the nations agreed to maintain the graves of foreign soldiers within their borders, an ironic charitable change from catastrophe.

In addition to winning the war, the doughboy generation created the modern American army. The war changed the future for the sons of the doughboys. U.S. soldiers returned home, but the American military would return to Europe. The world did not become "safe for democracy." Instead, the vindictiveness of the peace terms resulted in the opposite and led to the rise of the Third Reich.

A generation later, with the doughboy appellation gone, sons of the AEF soldiers were GIs in the Second World War.

In 1919, Octaviano Ambrosio Larrazolo was the Republican governor of New Mexico. He was also a delegate to the New Mexico Constitutional Convention and was the first Mexican-American U.S. senator. His legislative action included pardoning Mexican soldiers who raided New Mexico, bilingual education, civil rights for Mexican immigrants in New Mexico and an income tax law.

Governor Larrazolo supported President Wilson's League of Nations. The United States took the lead in creating the coalition designed to prevent the costs and consequences of further international madness. Although it was a laudable attempt to ensure that disputes were resolved without war, it failed. The U.S. lack of involvement, for fear of an impact on sovereignty, is often blamed for that failure.

David Elias Grant of Abiqiu, Rio Arriba County, New Mexico, was the secretary to the military attaché, American Embassy, Madrid, Spain, in 1918–19. He wrote the following at the end of the war:

> *In a word, it may be said that while the soldiers in the field saw the play of armies…we in Madrid saw the play of nations. That play which depends very little on the belching of guns and the minutely timed offensives but lies in the comprehensive minds of statesmen and deals not with trenches but with the destiny of nations and the equilibrium of peoples.*
>
> *To New Mexico, the Great War should mark a renaissance, an awakening to the solemn duties as one of the American union. Thousands of her sons have been taken from their oblivion, have been shown the world outside of New Mexico's boundaries, have come to appreciate in part the progress of America. To these men the war has been an education and a great opportunity, and it must rebound in the attitude to their state and in their service as citizens if we only know to follow up the advantage we have gained.*

New Mexico doughboys highlighted here exhibit the importance of leadership in achieving the AEF's mission and withstood the most inhumane warfare to date. Many factors influence the fortunes of war, but leadership is the most important and can be a part of every soldier. Each story within these pages shows an ability to face challenges in extremely dangerous situations.

There were many examples of character, inspiration and self-motivation for officers, noncommissioned officers and private soldiers. They showed leadership ability for their regiment, companies, platoons and for themselves. *World War I New Mexico* celebrates citizen-soldiers as decisive leaders. Indeed, New Mexico's doughboys demonstrated extraordinary leadership and decision-making abilities while in extreme physical and emotional states of mind—when all was on the line.

The November 11, 1918 "victory" would end on September 1, 1939. On that day, the sky over Poland was blue before suddenly changing to gray. It was not clouds that darkened the sky—it was the *Luftwaffe*. The German air force dominated the sky over Poland. The planes appeared to come from the heavens, but instead they came from hell, starting the Second World War and ultimately ending millions of lives, including many New Mexican soldiers.

The note to readers contains a ghost story that started my interest in the First World War. Yet this book was written for different reasons. This project intended to contribute to the remembrance of the centenary as a milestone in world events. Moreover, it intended to describe New Mexico's doughboys in a compelling way, to convey ideas about their leadership and to provide the respect and honor those soldiers deserve. I hope this book achieves its goals.